I0876712

Mao

Jonathan Clements is the author of many books about China, including biographies of Confucius, Empress Wu, and the First Emperor; and histories of Beijing, the Silk Road, and the martial arts. He was the presenter of three seasons of *Route Awakening*, an award-winning television series for National Geographic about icons of Chinese history and culture, and was formerly a visiting professor at Xi'an Jiaotong University from 2013–19. His most recent books include *The Emperor's Feast: A History of China in Twelve Meals*, and *Rebel Island: The Incredible History of Taiwan.*

Mao

Jonathan Clements

First published by
Haus Publishing
4 Cinnamon Row
London SW11 3TW
www.hauspublishing.com

First published in 2006
This revised edition published in 2026

A CIP catalogue record for this book is available from the British Library

ISBN 978-1-914979-53-8
eISBN 978-1-914979-57-6

Typeset in Garamond by MacGuru Ltd

Printed in the UK by United Kingdom by Clays Ltd, Elcograf S.p.A.

The authorised representative in the EEA is:
Haus Publishing
Casella Postale 32
50037 San Piero a Sieve (Fi), Italy
gpsr@hauspublishing.com

FSC www.fsc.org
MIX
Paper | Supporting responsible forestry
FSC® C018072

Contents

For John Bains

A note on romanisation

For much of his life, Mao's name was written in English as Mao Tse-tung and China's capital as Peking, using the antiquated Wade–Giles romanisation system. The modernised Pinyin system, which spells the same words more like the way they are pronounced, as in Mao Zedong and Beijing, was introduced in 1958 at the fifth session of the First National People's Congress. Pinyin was the system I was taught, and is favoured today by the majority of China scholars. Since 2009, its utility has even been recognised on Taiwan, where it is now used in official documents. I only use non-standard romanisations where common pronunciation reflects accents, personal choices, dialects, or topolects of Chinese that differ, such as Hong Kong (which would be Xiang Gang in Mandarin), or Chiang Kai-shek (which would be Jiang Jieshi if shorn of his Zhejiang accent).

Preface

I have tried to leave the original text of this book, which told Mao's story in a concise, chronological narrative, as untouched as possible. Where I saw an opportunity to sneak in a clarification or anecdote, I have done so, particularly when I am able to draw upon some of the books published about Mao in the last few years.

In the twenty years since I wrote the first edition, the imagery of Chairman Mao has gained new currency in modern China, sometimes literally. In 2012, I found two ladies selling trinkets on a street corner in Xi'an. Their baskets included stacks of 'ghost money' – counterfeit cash for filial Chinese to burn on pyres in order to send gifts to their ancestors in the afterlife. It was designed in a reasonable facsimile of real-life 100-yuan notes, printed in red ink and bearing the image of Chairman Mao. Each promised to pay the bearer on demand the sum of ten million yuan, redeemable at the 'Bank of Hell'. I found it ironic that the man who had once tried to ban both money *and* superstition should endure as the figurehead on cash for use in the spirit world.

I bought a supposed fortune in ghost money for a knockdown price, since the women were trying to offload their Mao notes as fast as possible. Such realistic ghost money had recently been declared illegal, in a re-establishment of respect for Mao that would see a new edition of his *Selected Quotations* (the famous Little Red Book) republished a few

Counterfeit money from the Bank of Hell, designed for burning.

months later. The following October, when I went looking for ghost money again, I could only buy notes bearing the face of the King of Hell. I would keep my Mao money for a decade, until I was persuaded to burn it on camera for William Shatner's *The UnXplained* to demonstrate how to turn my ancestors into millionaires.

Only two months after I bought the last of the Mao ghost money on the street, China's new president Xi Jinping delivered a stirring speech about his plans for the nation during what would turn out to be his lifelong term in office. He was determined, he said, for the Chinese Communist Party to celebrate its centenary in 2021 without any slanders or smears committed against it by hostile forces peddling an incorrect version of history. In doing so, he used the phrase 'historical nihilism' (*lishi xuwuzhuyi*), a term that has come to colour huge areas in subsequent discourse.

Thereafter, if I described myself as a historian, people

became noticeably jumpy. There was, after all, now a hotline for concerned citizens to call if they encountered anyone suspected of harming the reputation of the Communist Party and its role in creating the new China. History was now whatever the Party said it was, which has effectively criminalised anyone who dares to question it.

Chairman Mao remained the Communist Party's most visible and enduring icon. His face looks down on Tiananmen Square from a huge portrait on its north side. Despite a purge of many of his statues in the progressive 2000s, there are still plenty of them to go round. Lip service to the Great Helmsman is still a regular feature of public discourse, although ironically those hardliners who describe themselves as true Maoists are often silenced or censored, lest they dig up an unpleasantly contrary saying from China's most famous leader. With a shifting and slippery identity, the Chinese Communist Party relies upon the image of Mao as its go-to logo and poster-boy – a lodestone as it sails through troubled times. 'Without the cult of personality for Mao Zedong,' commented one activist in 2009, 'our Communist Party might have remained a sheet of loose sand and [we] would have remained groping in the darkness. To destroy Mao's cult of personality is to destroy the spirit of the Communist Party.'[1]

In other words: Mao is the Communist Party. The Communist Party is Mao. Questioning Mao's history is tantamount to questioning the Communist Party's right to rule.

Jonathan Clements, 2026

Early Life

Today, the Hunan village of Shaoshan, an hour's drive outside metropolitan Changsha, has been awarded the prestigious quintuple 'A' rating otherwise reserved for internationally famous destinations like the Tomb of the First Qin Emperor (home to the Terracotta Warriors) and the Forbidden City. A park-and-ride scheme attempts to filter the traffic jams off the highway, forcing most visitors to leave their vehicles on the outskirts to be bussed into the town proper.

You can poke around the beige-walled farmhouse where Chairman Mao spent the first seventeen years of his life – a venue that attracts long, snaking queues. From there, it is ten minutes' walk to the newer town square, dominated by a statue of the town's most famous son, at whose bronze feet visitors are encouraged to leave the elaborate and recyclable wreaths that are a thriving business for the local florists.

They are not the only residents to benefit from the twenty million annual visitors to Shaoshan, where one in every three locals now works in Mao-related tourism. Tripadvisor makes the unlikely claim that Shaoshan boasts eighty-two sites of tourist interest, including Mao's childhood school, his parents' tomb, the Mao family ancestral hall, a 'forest' of stone slabs carved with his poetry, a pond he once looked at, and restaurants serving Mao's red braised pork, a dish for which he only expressed a preference long

Tourists flock to Mao's childhood home in Shaoshan.

after he had left his home province behind.[1] Stretching the patience of even the most credulous Party faithful, visitors are also ushered around a cave with water dripping from the roof, which is supposedly close by to a villa where Mao once lived for a whole fortnight.

Such distractions reflect the way in which historical memory can be twisted and carnivalised – a swarm of Party faithful and performative Communists descending on an entirely humdrum town in the Chinese countryside, purely because its most famous son went on to become the leader of the nation. The 'humble' farmhouse where Mao grew up is actually quite large – three or four times the size of my own childhood home in the degenerate West. It made me wonder if, had things worked out only slightly differently, the Mao family might have ended up as one of those ousted or executed by Communist rebels who might have seen them as wealthy 'landlords'. It was, perhaps, lucky for the young Mao Zedong that his revolutionary activities took him far from home, before anyone asked too many questions about his background.

*

Mao Zedong was born in China's southern province of Hunan, in the peasant village of Shaoshan, on 26 December 1893. His father was Mao Rensheng, a labourer's son. When he was sixteen, Mao Rensheng was forced by heavy debts to join a local military battalion. He thereby earned enough money to buy a farm of his own, marrying Mao's mother, Wen Qimei, a religious-minded peasant girl. As befitted contemporary custom among the poor, she did not even have a name: *Qimei* means 'Seventh Sister'.

According to Chinese astrology, Mao was born in the year of the snake. Tradition held that his life would therefore be dominated by concern over financial matters, that he would be a nocturnal person given to working late at night, unconventional but politically minded, adept at befriending strangers, and preferring a quiet home life without disturbances. In later years, Mao would come to manifest all these characteristics although, as a good Communist, he set no store by superstition.

Although Mao would play up his peasant origins, he was relatively well-off by local standards. He was reared by his mother's family until he was eight – a sign that there was already trouble between his parents, and he was taught to address his uncle as Adopted Father. Already, he was expected to help in the fields, a duty that became more onerous when he moved back to be with his father. His father's land was twice the size of the average holdings in the area, stretching over two and a half acres of rice paddies, with a small cluster of forests, and a pond near the farmhouse that brimmed with lotus flowers.

As a farmer's son, Mao grew up with an immediate, innate appreciation of a truth that better-off Communist scholars would have to learn: land is a means of production. Every harvest time, the wet, swampy terraces of the rice fields would bring forth a new crop (in the hotter, wetter regions of the south, this could happen twice a year), and the land holding was large enough and prosperous enough that Mao's father was able to sell surplus produce, saving enough money to buy another acre, and then to hire two farmhands. In later life, Mao would claim that he was scandalised at the thought that, in times of hardship, his father was able to make more money by raising his prices and capitalising on the misfortune of others. However, Mao made little mention of such misgivings until his thirties.

The hired workers did not have fields of their own. Instead, they toiled long hours under the hot sun, calf-deep in insect-infested water, shoving new rice plants into a miasma of mud and human waste, or cutting them free once more with sickles. It was back-breaking work that occupied a sizeable portion of the Chinese population, and nor was the landowner's family excluded. The workers were only 'help'. Mao's father and mother could often be found out in the fields themselves, and the young Mao Zedong was expected to join them.

For the modern, Western reader, Mao's childhood must seem tough. Like other peasant boys, he was expected to lend a hand as soon as he was able, initially simply running errands between the house and fields, or watching over the cattle. He also worked in the fields, although his father had other plans for him.

In an age when the average Chinese peasant could expect to earn perhaps ten silver dollars a year, Mao's father amassed a fortune of nearly $3,000. He had done so by pouring his profits into improvements on the farm, using it to buy mortgages on other land and to buy surplus grain from poorer neighbours that he could sell at a profit 30 miles away in Xiangtan.

Mao despised his father's miserly attitude, although he would grow up to inherit it himself. But Mao's father was prepared to put some of his wealth to good use investing in his son's future. When Mao was eight, he was sent away to school, where he learned to read and write, as generations of Chinese children had before him, from classical Chinese texts.

Mao's generation was the last to be educated under the Confucian system that had dominated China for centuries. This system recognised only one form of learning as worthwhile: a mastery of the ancient classics set down by Confucius and his successors over 2,000 years earlier. Consequently, Mao and his fellow students pored over large-print versions of the classics, which used many of the complex ideograms that still formed the Chinese language in the nineteenth century. The children studied Confucian sayings such as: 'By nature, we are similar. By nurture, we differ greatly,'[2] reciting and writing the first thousand characters by rote, then a list of Chinese surnames, then other books thought to instil classical virtues in the young. At the apex of the Imperial education system were the draconian civil-service exams, which involved arduous hours locked in a room reproducing selected classical passages from memory and composing a stylised essay. Although this theoretically allowed some low-born students to ascend to the higher levels of government, the emphasis on rote learning of ancient treatises helped encourage a government and society that remained mired in the past.

China, written in its native language, is *Zhong-guo*, the 'Middle Kingdom', a vestige of the imperial era when the ruler of China believed himself to be the centre of the entire world. Confucian philosophy held that the emperor was chosen as a heavenly envoy on earth, a mortal representative of an unknowable divine order, charged with making sacrifices and meting out justice to ensure that the gods in heaven remained placated.

Confucianism, however, was not much interested in gods. Several of its contending schools suggested, or at least implied, that the gods were merely allegories, handy tools for thinking about the universe, but not to be taken literally. A true Confucian should not concern himself with thoughts of the divine and the supernatural, but instead concentrate on the world around him, honouring his parents, elders, and superiors, and caring for his children, juniors, and inferiors (which included women). If everyone observed these proprieties, so went the logic, then the world would be a harmonious place, with the emperor himself at its hierarchical summit. This system depended on the integrity of the state. At numerous points in Chinese history, the crops had failed, barbarians had raided at the borders, or natural disasters had struck the nation. At such times, if he was unable to cope with the difficulties, the emperor was thought to have lost the Mandate of Heaven, that divine right to rule conferred upon him by the gods. If he did not atone for his nation's supposed misdeeds, then his reign would be forfeit.

At the time of the birth of Mao, the last acknowledged change in mandate had come in 1644, when the ailing Ming dynasty was overthrown by internal conflicts. The ultimate victors were outsiders, Manchurian tribesmen from the north, who seized the country, married into its aristocracy, and proclaimed themselves as a new dynasty, the Qing.

Despite some revolts and border conflicts, the Manchus retained hold of China for 200 years, but the latter part of the nineteenth century saw China under attack from all sides. While the ruling class continued to assure themselves that they were the masters of the world, the 'barbarian' kingdoms of the West took increasing liberties. Intent on maintaining a drug trade into south China, Great Britain embarked upon the Opium Wars, which forced the Chinese to make diplomatic and mercantile concessions, including the unwelcome opening of several new treaty ports. Other nations seized coastal towns, and the Chinese were forced into unfavourable trading agreements with the French, Italians, Russians, and Germans. As the Manchu government lost hold on power, peasants in the hinterland rose up in revolt, most notably in the Taiping Rebellion, a fourteen-year civil war that cost more than twenty million lives. When Mao was two years old, his country suffered another defeat, this time by Japan, whose modern fleet of ironclad, steam-powered ships wiped out the ill-disciplined, poorly trained northern Chinese navy.

There were several attempts to revitalise China, to wake it from its centuries of smug slumber, and to bring it into line with the industrial powers. Many, however, suffered the fate of the abortive Tongzhi Restoration of 1873, in which attempts to modernise were thwarted by bureaucracy, political inertia, and officials' lack of practical knowledge. China's neighbour Japan had swiftly learned its lesson after ill treatment at the hands of imperialistic invaders, and dispatched missions to the West to learn new skills in law, science, engineering, and medicine. In China however, any education that did not involve the memorisation of the Confucian classics was not deemed worthwhile. Civil servants and government officials made all the important decisions, and one could not become a civil servant without completing the time-honoured Confucian syllabus. Mao would claim in later life to despise the writings of Confucius, but they formed a large part of his education, far more so than his often sketchy understanding of Marxist thinkers like Lenin and Engels.

In a China starved of doctors and still reliant on traditional medicine, the infant mortality rate was high. Four of Mao's siblings died young, although his brothers Zemin (born 1895) and Zetan (born 1903) survived. The family also adopted Mao's cousin, Zejian, a niece of his father's. As is still common today with Chinese families, a single word was common to all the siblings of a particular generation, in this case *ze*, or 'anointed', an attempt to magically 'rehydrate' the Mao family's supposed deficiency in water, one of the five Chinese elements. This supposed problem had been identified by a fortune teller at the time of Mao's birth – a piece of local folklore that ensured the next generation began its filial duties before it could even walk, with a name that helped improve the family's fortunes.

Mao's father hoped that his eldest son would put his education to immediate use on the estate, calculating accounts with the aid of an abacus. But in learning to read, Mao also gained access to books that were not part of the school syllabus, particularly the works of the fourteenth-century novelist Luo Guanzhong. Luo is attributed with the authorship of two of China's most enduringly popular novels. He is believed to be the sole author of *Romance of the Three Kingdoms*, a semi-historical tale of the collapse of China's Han dynasty in the third century CE, and the jockeying for supremacy of wily politicians. With Shi Nai'an, he is also believed to have written *Water Margin*, a fictionalised account of a group of noble-minded rebels who hid in the marshes of Liang Shan Po and fought a war of attrition against the corrupt officials of the late twelfth-century

Song dynasty. An old Chinese proverb warns: 'Don't let the young read *Water Margin*. Don't let the old read *Three Kingdoms*', for the former encourages rebellion against authority, and the latter cunning diplomatic schemes. Typically, Mao read them both, along with *Journey to the West*, the story of a divine monkey king who embarks upon a long march to a distant destination, evading his enemies through trickery and deceit.

While the machinations of the *Three Kingdoms* would inspire Mao in later life, as a child it was the other books that held his attention. Reading in secret in his room by the light of a hidden lamp, he was inspired to stand up more to his father.

Aged ten, Mao also rebelled against his school, avoiding class but fearing to return home, since his father would then realise he was playing truant. That, at least, is how his later Communist Party hagiographers would paint his youthful disobedience. Less forgiving observers might instead have noted a spoilt, rebellious nature that would lead him to leave, or be asked to leave, three other schools. Since both school and home would mean punishment, the young Mao instead set out in what he believed to be the direction of the nearest town. He was gone for three days, inadvertently describing a rough circle around his birthplace and returning to his irate parents.

As Mao entered his teens, China was forced to confront further assaults on its traditions. In 1905, the Confucian exam system was abolished. At the very age that Mao would be expecting to put his classical education to use, he was informed that it was no longer required. The shock would reverberate throughout Mao's career, becoming the cornerstone of both his politics and his insecurities. The fact that, in 1906, the emperor proclaimed that Confucius should be worshipped at the highest level, on a par with Heaven and Earth themselves, was scant consolation. Faced with such about-faces regarding the foundations of their culture, it is unsurprising that youths of Mao's generation embraced adolescent rebellion with a passion.

'When I was about thirteen my father invited many guests to his home,' he recalled, 'and when they were present a dispute arose between the two of us. My father denounced me before the whole group, calling me lazy and useless. This infuriated me. I cursed him and left the house. My mother ran after me and tried to persuade me to return. My father also pursued me, cursing at the same time as he commanded me to come back. I reached the edge of a pond and threatened to jump in if he came any nearer.'[3]

The damage was already done. Merely by standing up to his father, Mao had scored a victory, causing his father to lose face before his guests. Mao's father demanded that his son kneel and bow before him in supplication, touching the ground with his forehead. Mao immediately offered to drop to one knee only, and insisted that his father also promise not to beat him in retaliation. 'Thus the war ended,' he said, remembering the story as an older revolutionary, 'and from it I learned that when I defended my rights by open rebellion my father relented, but when I remained weak and submissive he only beat me more.'[4]

The adult Mao framed his early home life as a revolutionary struggle. 'There were two "parties" in the family. One was my father, the Ruling Power. The Opposition was made up of myself, my mother, my brother, and sometimes even the labourer[s]. In the "united front" of the Opposition, however, there was a difference of opinion. My mother advocated a policy of indirect attack. She criticised any overt display of emotion, and attempts at open rebellion against the Ruling Power. She said it was not the Chinese Way.'[5]

Father and son were soon at odds again, in 1907, when Mao was presented with a fiancée. The story seems steeped in unmentioned scandal – the fourteen-year-old Mao was 'betrothed' to a twenty-year-old woman known only as 'Miss Luo'. The woman moved into the family home, where she was expected to work in the fields, but Mao refused to have anything to do with her. Gossip in Mao's later life alleged that Luo was really intended as a concubine to Mao's father. Mao himself soon left the family home, but Miss Luo stayed behind and died later that year. Mao's mother left, too, going to live with her brother's family: a sign of marital separation. At her funeral years later, Mao would openly accuse his father of betraying marital responsibility.[6]

Mao would have three other wives during his lifetime. In 1920 he would marry Yang Kaihui, who bore him three children but was executed in 1930. By then, he had already been married for two years to He Zizhen, mother of five other children, whom he divorced in 1938. His last and most famous wife was Jiang Qing, whom he married in 1938. She would bear one son, and they remained at least

Mao photographed as a young man, around 1910.

officially together until his death in 1976.

Despite Mao's later claims of his contempt for his father (a hatred gently excised from many Chinese accounts, but present in Western interviews), the man he painted as a penny-pinching tyrant still paid his ever-increasing school fees, even when it became clear that the farmer's son would not return to his home village. Mao had read *Words of Warning to a Prosperous Age* by Zheng Guanying, a book that outlined the troubles China would face if it did not embrace modernisation, and he was swayed by its message. With the continued support of his father, he followed his mother to the neighbouring county, where he attended a bigger school that only inspired him to move further away from his origins.

The Republican Revolution

Perhaps Mao's father was prepared to send Mao to better schools because he could afford it; 1909 was a good year for business. The mighty River Yangtze burst its banks on two occasions, extensively flooding Hunan and the neighbouring province of Hubei, and destroying much of the year's crops. The governor of Hunan attempted to limit rice exports to other provinces, but he was outvoted by the local merchants, who saw the chance for profit, and the British consul, who insisted on a strict enforcement of recent trade treaties. Within a few months, most of the small landholders had sold or eaten their remaining crops, and the price of rice skyrocketed.

For someone like Mao's father, with surplus grain to sell, the increase in prices was highly lucrative. For peasants who had already lost their homes and possessions to flooding, left penniless by the destruction of the crops that formed their sole income, it was a disaster. By April 1910, the price of rice had tripled, and people were starving in the streets of the provincial capital, Changsha. Several sources, including the Japanese consul, confirmed rumours that a desperate couple had committed suicide, leaving their children to eat cakes made from mud. It was a human-interest story of powerful weight, and as the news spread, a local mob began rioting for food. The riot soon turned into an attack and looting of foreign concessions in the town, particularly the riverboat companies, whose steam vessels had whisked all the local produce away to other markets, or distant warehouses from which it could be resold to the starving.

Out of harm's way, Mao heard second-hand of the carnage that ensued, the international incident that led to the evacuation of British citizens by gunboats, and the irate demands for reparations from the American consulate. In the aftermath, the peasant rebels were executed, but the local gentry who had encouraged them merely received token punishment: a reversible 'reduction in rank' that was of little impact to their lives or standing.

'It made a deep impression on me,' said Mao. 'Most of the other students sympathised with the "insurrectionists" but ... they did not understand that it had any relation to their own lives. They were merely interested in it as an exciting incident. I never forgot it. I felt that there with the rebels were ordinary people like my own family, and I deeply resented the injustice of the treatment given to them.'[1]

Ever since the Manchu conquest in 1644, rumours had persisted of an underground resistance, seeking to overthrow the invaders and restore a true 'Chinese' ruler. Such societies included the Plum Blossom, supposedly formed by Ming dynasty loyalists at the fall of Taiwan, and the Eight Trigrams, from which the Boxer movement grew. There were many 'secret societies' in China, some little more than gentlemen's clubs, others athletic organisations or primitive forms of bank. Since the eighteenth century, many of the societies purporting to be anti-government were simply anti-law: covers for criminal endeavour.

In Huashi, only 25 miles away from Mao's new home,

an argument escalated between a landowner and a group of local peasants, who were emboldened by their shared membership of a secret society. As had happened with the Changsha riots, the establishment favoured the richer plaintiff, but this time the peasants did not submit. Instead, a group of men hid out in the wilderness, claiming that they were inspired by the Boxer rebels in the north, and that they would resist the corruption of the government.

The Boxers, unknown to Mao until long after the original event, had held Beijing's European compounds to ransom in 1900. An offshoot of one of China's many secret societies, the Yihe Quan (Righteous and Harmonious Fist) organisation was a martial-arts group who believed that Chinese mysticism could give them supernatural powers.

On the understanding that it was better to unite against a common enemy than to fight each other, the Manchu government gave tacit support to the Boxer rebels, even sending a detachment of imperial troops to blockade Western peacekeepers advancing from the coast. Eventually, the besieged Europeans at Beijing were relieved by a multinational force of foreign troops, the imperial family lost massive face, and further embarrassing reparations were extorted from the Chinese.

News could travel slowly in turn-of-the-century China, with garbled accounts of the Boxers taking several years to drift southwards. The Huashi rebels, like the Boxers before them, claimed that their martial-arts prowess made them invulnerable: a boast swiftly revealed to be untrue when their ringleader was beheaded by government enforcers.

Unrest was growing all over China, a fact that even Mao could now appreciate, since the danger was drifting ever closer to those he knew. As further famines and shortages gripped the nation in 1911, Mao's father complained that he was losing profits because one of his grain shipments had been seized by thieves. Although Mao disapproved of the crime, he knew that the thieves were hungry, and that the shortage of grain was largely caused by men like his father, and the inability of the state to ensure that emergency supplies could be shipped from neighbouring prefectures.

Mao, meanwhile, continued with his studies. He moved to Changsha, observing like many others of his generation that China's former enemy, Japan, seemed to be setting the model for modernisation. While China was forced to bow to Western powers, Japan had transformed itself and met the foreigners on their own terms, even defeating Russia in a war in 1905. 'At the time,' Mao said, 'I knew and felt the beauty of Japan, and felt something of her pride and might in this ... victory over Russia.'[2] Japan's modernisation had saved it from the aggression of the Western powers, and Mao wanted something similar for China. But while Mao continued to believe fervently in the need for China to emulate Japan in embracing the new disciplines of science and engineering, his own abilities seemed ironically much more traditional. He focused on history and literature, taking particular interest in 2,000-year-old stories of China's First Emperor, who had unified the disparate country and imposed draconian schemes that helped forge China the nation. Mao still supported the imperial system, unaware that there was any alternative, but before long he would be keenly following the activities of revolutionaries in south China.

Sometimes it is easy to forget how little the youthful Mao knew of the outside world. It was only in Changsha as a young man that he saw his first newspaper, a journal not of legendary deeds, like his favourite novels, but of actual events taking place in his country. On reading of a failed revolt in Canton, he put up a poster at his new school, naming three famous revolutionaries as the ideal men to run a new government.

Mao's chosen president was Sun Yat-sen, leader of the anti-Manchu agitators. But Mao's other two candidates both supported the imperial structure: aged eighteen, Mao sought a change in regime, but not necessarily the removal of the emperor system. Like many others at the time, he simply believed that the mandate of the Manchus had come to an end, and it was time for China to be ruled by the Chinese.

For more than two hundred years, adult Chinese had been forced to wear their hair in a Manchu 'queue', the front of their heads shaved forward of the ears, the hair at the back gathered into a long braid. It was the ultimate symbol of their position with relation to the Manchus, the alteration of their heads into replicas of horses' tails, with the consequent acknowledgement that they were the beasts of burden, and the Manchus were their masters. Refusal to adopt the queue had previously been an offence punishable by death. Now, rebellious schoolboys like Mao and his

A reformer cuts off the queue of a peasant.

associates cut off their queues in protest. In an early precursor of the elder Mao's steely resolve, he and his friends also hunted down fellow scholars who had offered support but backed away from the act, hacking off their braids. It was a typical teenage rebellion, designed to unite the young and horrify the old. But in a climate of revolution, it only added fuel to the fire.

News drifted in from the capital that the authorities would make concessions. A move towards constitutional government, promised since 1908, lost its lustre when it was found to mainly comprise Manchu princes. Assurances of a plan to modernise transport, namely the construction of a national railway system, initially sounded like the kind of development Mao would have wanted, but the government intended to pay for it by taking massive loans from abroad. Rather than liberating and encouraging movement and trade among the Chinese, the new railways would merely allow the hated Western powers an even greater hold on China.

Would-be revolutionaries like Mao found a cause on 9 October 1911, when fighting broke out in Beijing. An explosion was caused by a bomb going off while still being assembled, and Manchu investigators uncovered another secret society preparing to attack the government. Several ringleaders were executed, but the attitude of the government caused further repercussions elsewhere. The Manchus had always been outnumbered by their Chinese subjects, the potential for revolution constantly held in check by an inclusive system that offered the faithful positions of authority in the government of the conquerors. That system, however, had been fatally undermined by the previous years of defeats and embarrassments; the Chinese were less likely to be swayed by offers of careers in a government that could not even control its own country.

Native Chinese troops in a nearby garrison turned on their officers. Notably, the first division to rebel were engineers: the product of one of the progressive disciplines that the Manchus had spurned for so long. Claiming to be working in support of home rule for the Chinese, the troops killed any officers who did not agree. Manchus in the vicinity were forced to flee, while rumours drifted into the capital of lynchings in the countryside.

Even in the hinterland, where Mao found himself, the disaffected were numerous enough that real revolution appeared to be in the offing. Representatives from the mutineers arrived in Changsha, and one was permitted to address Mao's school assembly, urging the boys to support the foundation of a Chinese republic. Caught up in the fervour, Mao and several friends resolved to join the republican army, but even as they prepared to catch a ferry downstream to volunteer, the revolution came to them.

High-ranking Manchu officers, realising that the Changsha garrison was probably full of revolutionaries, had wisely deployed it elsewhere, leaving only 600 men in a barracks just outside the city's east gate. Since rebellious soldiers presented a greater danger to the immediate security of the state than rioting peasants, the 600 troops were now ordered to hand over their ammunition.

Mao claimed to have witnessed what happened next, although his dramatic account does not match those of others. It is known, from dispatches of the British consul in Changsha, that the revolution got off to a messy start, with arsonists setting a blaze inside the city gates in an attempt to get the gates to open and allow the radicals among the troops to seize the city. Although this plan failed, by the following day radical sympathisers had won over the guards of the ammunition store, and the soldiers were able to re-arm. The following day, the troops entered the city and marched to the quarters of the governor, who appeared to have fled. They took control of the city with no resistance offered by any of the city's defenders.

Mao's version, however, as retold fifteen years later, gives the masses a starring role. He said he saw the 'great battle' from a high vantage point, and witnessed the inspiring sight of Chinese labourers storming the city gates while the rebel soldiers fought the Manchu loyalists. Mao's account only matches that of the British consul towards the end, when both acknowledge the sudden appearance of the rebels' flag. It was white, and emblazoned with the single character *Han*, a symbol of the native Chinese whom the Manchus had once conquered and who had now risen up.[3]

With local victory secure, the rebels were now faced with the need to impose their own order. In Wuchang, the site of the original mutiny, the military nature of the resistance was acknowledged by the election of a military leader. The soldiers chose one Li Yuanhong, a brigadier highly regarded by not only by the original mutineers, but also by those who had been forced to join them, since he was both a reluctant convert to their cause and an unwilling leader.

In Mao's Changsha, the situation was far more chaotic. Power was shared via an uneasy truce between Tan Yankai, an upper-class reformist, and Jiao Dafeng, a local hero with strong ties to the criminal underworld. Far from restoring order, the rival factions continued fighting, until a few days later, when the local hero and his assistant turned up dead. Mao saw the bodies lying in the street, and took from it a lesson in revolution: that a military victory would not necessarily remove all enemies, merely the ones that are most obvious. 'They were not bad men,' he commented, 'and [they] had some revolutionary intentions. [They were killed because] they were poor and represented the interests of the oppressed. The landlords and the merchants were dissatisfied with them.'[4]

Although the farmers and labourers had played an important part in the revolution in Changsha, their idea of reform was not the same as the landlords'. While the population of Changsha was united in its desire to see a change in the Manchu regime, the upper classes still wanted to hold onto power. With Jiao Dafeng gone, responsibility for the city fell to Tan Yankai, who was far more to the liking of the elite, and who immediately imposed a fierce and violent rule.[5]

Similar events took place in several other Hunanese towns, but not with the same degree of revolutionary success. In fact, only four large towns were unequivocally rebel territory. Others were the site of struggles or rebel defeats. To a certain extent, the rebellion benefited from the relative slowness of communications in China, since rumours of rebel successes elsewhere took so long to debunk that they had often inspired other rebellions closer to home.

The Manchus went on the defensive. The emperor's regents issued a proclamation on his behalf, promising amnesty to anyone in the rebel provinces of Hubei and Hunan. Seemingly attempting to capitalise on the ruler's youth (the emperor was only six years old at the time), the proclamation offered further reforms, and acknowledged that unless something was done, the Mandate of Heaven would truly be lost.

But even as the emperor's decree promised leniency, forces loyal to the Manchus were attacking China's second city, Nanjing. If the troops found any man without the mandatory 'queue', they killed him on the spot. For youths such as Mao who had already cut off their braids and openly declared their defiance, there was little option. With the struggle between rebels and loyalists still too close to call, he joined the revolutionary army for real.

Mao served as a soldier in Changsha's revolutionary militia for less than six months. While factions within the republican revolutionaries continued to duel and argue on the streets, Mao was largely confined to his garrison's barracks, the converted Courts of Justice, where he undertook errands for the officers. Like one of the elite he supposedly despised, he drew the line at carrying water, and would use part of his allowance to pay his fellow soldiers to do it for him. Meanwhile, he won over many of the poor, uneducated labourers by offering to write letters for them. As someone who could not only read, but had read more than one book, he was regarded by his fellow soldiers as something of an intellectual.

While Mao and his fellow soldiers whiled away the days in Changsha, the revolution proceeded elsewhere. Nanjing was seized by the rebels, and revolutionaries in Beijing secured the emperor's promise to abdicate. However, the conflict of interests between military and intellectuals that Mao had witnessed in Changsha threatened to break out into a civil war as rebel factions split between the northern military men, led by the high-ranking officer Yuan Shikai, and the southern rebels, revolutionaries, secret societies, and reformists, led by Sun Yat-sen.

The child of a poor farming family in Guangdong

province, Sun had spent the years 1880–83 in Hawaii, in the care of his elder brother. Returning to China and graduating as a doctor of medicine in 1892, he took up revolutionary politics, founding the Xing Zhong (Revive China) society in 1894. Between 1895 and 1911, he was involved in up to ten attempts to incite revolution in south China, operating largely from exile.

It seemed as if Mao's fellows would now have to fight a new war, not against Manchus, but against northerners who did not recognise the southerners' right to rule. But even as demonstrations were organised against Yuan Shikai, the rebel leaders struck a deal. Sun Yat-sen was proclaimed president of the newly republican China, and the emperor officially abdicated on 12 February 1912.

Two days later, Sun Yat-sen resigned; his selection had been an interim compromise, but he was powerless without Yuan Shikai, to whom he had promised the presidency. One of the first Chinese commoners to attain high office without a degree, Yuan had failed his civil-service exams, but won high office after serving in Korea and during the Sino-Japanese war. He had gained high rank by default when his division of the Chinese army was the only one to survive the Boxer Rebellion, and oversaw attempts at modernisation before being fired by the imperial regents in 1908. He derived his power from his control of the military, which trumped any ideological claims that Sun Yat-sen might have over the will of the people.

Yuan Shikai duly assumed the presidency himself, backed by his army, and with the momentous end of the

Sun Yat-sen (1866–1925).

centuries of Manchu rule and the proclamation of a republican China, Mao believed that things had changed. Before long, revolutionary battalions all over the country were being advised that their job was done, and they could go back to their homes. 'Thinking the revolution was over,' he said, 'I ... decided to return to my books. I had been a soldier for half a year.'[6]

The Thwarted Reformers

A new order did not necessarily ensure that Mao would find somewhere to fit in. In all the excitement of post-revolutionary China, there were so many opportunities that he did not know where to turn. He toyed with the idea of becoming a lawyer, and wrote to his father in search of tuition fees. Influenced by the theories of Marx and the chatter of his friends, he decided that economics might be more useful in the New China, and signed up for an economics course, only to tire of it, apply to a higher-level college, and then drop out when he found that it was mostly taught in English, which he did not understand. Although Mao was a theoretical revolutionary, the urban, 'bourgeois' (middle-class) revolution had already left him behind. Without English, he was not going to get anywhere. He thought of being a policeman, and registered for an examination, but was soon distracted by an advert for a soap-making school.

He finally found something that suited him in spring 1913, in an advertisement for teacher training at the Hunan Fourth Provincial Normal School. 'I read with interest of its advantages: no tuition [fees] required and cheap board and cheap lodging. Two of my friends were also urging me to enter, they wanted my help in preparing entrance essays.'[1] In fact, they wanted Mao to *cheat* on their behalf, and he did, writing the required essays for all three of them, and thereby qualifying for the course thrice over.

Portrait of Mao, around 1913.

Mao studied education for almost five years, learning about the world even as it changed around him. The period of his college education roughly coincided with the First World War, but the most important event to influence Mao's own development was the 1917 revolution in Russia in which the ruling Romanov dynasty was overthrown by Communist agitators. Mao saw many parallels with China's situation: pre-revolutionary Russia was ruled by an emperor, humiliated in a conflict with Japan, and was slowly starving its citizenry in the name of commerce (it was not lost on Mao that tsarist Russia continued to export grain, even while millions of its citizens were starving).

Mao's reading widened, taking in Chinese translations of Western books alongside classical Chinese texts and histories. But most prominent among his chosen reading matter were works by and about Lord Shang, who, in the fourth century BCE, had established a ruthless code known as Legalism. Unlike the benevolent rule of the ancient sage Confucius, Legalism suggested that people were inherently selfish, and needed to be bullied into doing what was right. It might be regarded as the dark side of Chinese philosophy, twisting the emphasis on harmony and obedience into a cult of dictatorship.

Meanwhile, in the capital, the hopes of a new China were fast receding. The emperor had abdicated, but President Yuan Shikai inherited many of the same problems, including the threat from foreign powers and a backward bureaucracy resistant to modernisation. Ideologically, China was splitting in two, between the northern prefectures that followed Yuan Shikai's thinly disguised continuation of Manchu order, and the southern prefectures, many of which still supported Sun Yat-sen. Sun, for his part, formed the Guomin Dang (Nationalist Party), often known by its initials under the old romanisation system: KMT.

China's far south and south-west remained semi-independent of Beijing's control, but after a failed attempt to fight Yuan Shikai, the Nationalist Party was banned all over China, forcing many of its leaders back into exile. In Mao's native Hunan, the pro-Nationalist governor Tan Yankai was ousted at the instigation of the Beijing government in 1913, and replaced with the conservative Tang Xiangming. 'Butcher' Tang, as he soon became known, conducted a series of ruthless purges of Nationalist supporters, conducting mass executions and the torture of suspected sympathisers. Five thousand people are believed to been killed during his three-year reign, including many members of the deposed Tan Yankai's government.

However, the Nationalists did not go away, and nor did the problems facing China from outside. Matters came to a head in 1915 when Yuan Shikai was presented with a series of Twenty-One Demands by the Japanese government, imposing further indignities on China – such as a demand for the former German colony of Shandong and shared rights with the Russians in Manchuria.

Mao was incensed at the continued abuse of China at foreign hands, railing in a poem about Japan and Russia that: 'The east sea holds island savages / In the northern mountains hate-filled enemies abound.'[2] Predicting that China would be completely crushed unless it resisted Japan, Mao wrote an article for *Xin Qingnian* (*New Youth*) magazine, in which he called for the Chinese to pay greater attention to sport and exercise in order to be ready to meet the challenge. His essay contained elements of both the 'superior man' analogies of Confucianism, and the earthy, physical concerns of socialism:

> Our nation is wanting in strength ... The military spirit has not been encouraged. The physical

> condition of our people deteriorates daily …
> The superior man's deportment is cultivated and agreeable, but one cannot say this about exercise. Exercise should be savage and rude. To charge on horseback amidst the clash of arms and to be ever-victorious; to shake the mountains by one's cries and the colours of the sky by one's roars of anger … has nothing to do with delicacy.[3]

Mao's early writings displayed characteristics that would persist throughout his life: whatever his argument, he would first ground it in local anecdotes or tales of Chinese tradition. Even when arguing for the application of Western ideas or techniques, he would try to frame them in a form familiar to the Chinese. This was both a handy rhetorical device for winning over local audiences, and a means of hiding his own shortcomings. Mao's early years reading the Chinese classics would have been otherwise wasted, but this way he was at least able to put his discredited education to some use.

Yuan Shikai proclaimed himself emperor in December 1915, leading to his violent ejection from office, and a series of local uprisings against his supporters. Hunan was a particular centre of trouble, since its geographically central location left it open to attacks both from northern supporters of the Beijing regime, and from southern Nationalists. The local government established in the 1911 uprising fell apart; and Governor Tang fled with much of the local tax revenue, while his lesser officers were rounded up and executed by the resurgent Nationalists.

Yuan Shikai, the provisional president of the Chinese Republic, 1913.

The outgoing regime had committed terrible atrocities, but Mao wrote that the governor had been much maligned: 'Driving him out was an injustice, and the situation now is growing more and more chaotic. [He] was here for three years, and he ruled by the severe enforcement of strict laws ... Order was restored, and the peaceful times of the past were practically regained.' Mao went on to claim that during the rule of the man he had joined the local militia to put into power, 'The city of Changsha became so honest that lost belongings were left on the street for their owners.'[4] The phrase was an allusion to an old story about Confucius, which claimed similar utopian conditions when the sage was briefly given control of a town.

Mao set up a strangely secretive group that both debated big issues of the day and indulged in hearty exercise. His recruitment of people through a pseudonymous bulletin was initially treated as a suspicious attempt to find female companionship, but was allowed to continue when it was found to be harmless. While Mao was a diligent student, he was also pathologically intense. In his student writings, we see elements of the same self-criticism that an older Mao would force his associates to undertake. Mao wrote to himself in his journal in 1915:

> You do not have the capacity for tranquillity. You are fickle and excitable. Like a woman preening herself, you know no shame. Your outside looks strong, but your inside is truly empty. Your ambitions for fame and fortune are not suppressed, and your sensual desire grows daily. You enjoy all hearsay and rumour, perturbing the spirit and misusing time, and generally delight in yourself.[5]

In 1917, Mao was voted Student of the Year by his classmates, and also elected head of the Students' Society, a body whose responsibilities included the arrangement of night school for local workers. Mao courted controversy by keeping the classes vocational, throwing out traditional rote-learning in favour of basic skills such as arithmetic and literacy. He also encouraged his workers in economic patriotism, urging them to support their nation by buying locally made goods.

When unrest broke out again in Hunan, Mao and his fellow students volunteered once more, patrolling with fake guns in the hope of discouraging disorder before it could arise. Before long, a new warlord was in charge, and Mao's school had been partly converted into barracks for some of his uncouth, violent soldiers. Mao graduated as a teacher in 1918, and the end of the First World War and China's humiliation thereafter were to have a radical effect on him.

Mao and some of his friends visited Professor Yang Changji, an influential tutor of his who was now in Beijing. A teacher who enjoyed the nickname 'Confucius' among his students, Professor Yang emphasised a sense of ethics and public duty. He had a strong background in classical Chinese rhetoric, but had also travelled in Britain, Germany, and Japan, and was unafraid of integrating modern ideas into his lessons. Inspired by Professor Yang's example, some of the students intended to head to France for further study, but Mao shied away. He claimed that responsibility lay partly with his mother, who was ill, and also that he could not afford the price of the boat-trip and language lessons. But Mao had managed to find funding before: it seems that his lack of progress in English made him doubt that French would be any easier.

Instead, Mao used Professor Yang's connections to get a lowly job at the library of Beijing University. His immediate

Mao's brother Zetan, his father, his uncle, and Mao himself, 1919.

boss was the co-editor of the *New Youth* magazine, but despite such prestigious company, Mao found his humble position frustrating. He earned half as much as a rickshawman and was forced to share a tiny living space with seven others. Mao soon returned home to Changsha, where his mother's ailing health was growing too bad to ignore.

Meanwhile, China's hopes of reasonable treatment in the wake of the First World War were dashed at the Paris Peace Conference. Since Shandong province had been occupied by Germany under the terms of unequal treaties, the Chinese expected it to be returned to them after Germany's defeat. Instead, they were forced to watch as it was handed to the Japanese, who had been one of the victorious Allied powers, and whose soldiers had occupied Shandong during the war. For many of Mao's generation, it was the final straw. Those who had supported the idea of Western-style liberalism now felt that the industrial nations saw China as another territory to carve apart. While Japan had somehow gained admittance to the club of exploitative powers, China was still one of the exploited.

Many disaffected Chinese revolutionaries turned their backs on Western ideas, preferring to take their chances with other theories. Mao was attracted initially to anarchism, with its stated aim of a harmonious, united world, in which people were equal, regardless of race, colour, or creed. It was an ideal philosophy for an underdog, and many of Mao's contemporaries embraced it as such, particularly since it was much easier to understand than Marxism: 'The world is ours, the nation is ours, society is ours. If we do not speak, who will speak? If we do not act, who will act?'[6]

News of the loss of Shandong led to riots all over China. On Sunday, 4 May 1919, a crowd of 3,000 gathered in front of the Gate of Heavenly Peace (Tiananmen) in the centre of Beijing and refused to leave, despite pleas from the chief of police. They were eventually incited by anarchists to attack the offices of the ministers thought responsible for the betrayal of China's interests, and in the ensuing struggle, several students were injured (one fatally) and another thirty-two were arrested.

Mao later wrote:

> Our Chinese people possess great inherent capacities! The more profound the oppression, the more powerful its reaction, and since this has been

accumulating for a long time, it will surely burst forth quickly. I venture to make a singular assertion: one day the reform of the Chinese people will be more profound than that of any other people, and the society of the Chinese people will be more radiant than that of any other people ... Our golden age, our age of glory and splendour, lies before us![7]

The Chinese Communist Party

Mao missed all the action of the May Fourth Movement, as it came to be known. While others of his generation were denouncing the Japanese and chanting before the Gate of Heavenly Peace, he was in Changsha, where Zhang Jingyao, the newest of a series of governors, cracked down on any violence not perpetrated by his own enforcers. After the flight of 'Butcher' Tang, Changsha had briefly been under the rule of its former governor Tan Yankai, before he was replaced once again, at Beijing's insistence, by Fu Liangzou, a local man who had previously been vice-minister of war in Beijing. Fu began his tenure in 1917 by sacking the officers in the local military who he did not trust. What seemed like a smart move immediately backfired: within three days he had a military insurrection on his hands, and then an invasion of a new army from the south. When the fighting was done, Hunan was back in the hands of Beijing sympathisers, and its new governor was Zhang 'the Venomous' Jingyao. Zhang turned out to be different to 'Butcher' Tang only in the scale of his atrocities – his men ranged far wider in their search for 'enemies', and Hunan lost another 21,000 lives to the acts of its supposed rulers.

With the new governor ever ready to mete out the death penalty for transgressions real and imagined, protests in Changsha took a more passive form, with a general boycott of

Japanese goods and services. Mao contributed to this protest by helping to form the Hunan United Students' Association. Over the summer of 1919, he could be found in Changsha diligently organising demonstrations and programmes that brought the revolutionary students together with the merchants and the workers. It is notable at the time that he associated largely with these people, rather than the rural peasants who he would claim to champion in later years. Mao began publishing a weekly newspaper, the *Xiang River Review*, with a reformist agenda, in which he published a series of articles outlining his plans for a new China.

Many of the scholars who had ignored Mao (some quite literally) when he was a librarian, found his ideas much more interesting when they were set down in print. Mao outlined ideas for women's rights, and even issued stern warnings about a coming alliance between Japan and Germany.

As other parts of China returned to calm, Hunan became a flashpoint for conflict. Beijing attempted to mollify the reformists again, but Zhang 'the Venomous' banned the Student Association. Mao pushed too far by publishing an editorial in which he accused the governor of attempting to censor free speech, and the *Xiang River Review* was shut down. In response, Mao formed part of a delegation that went to Beijing in an attempt to secure Zhang's dismissal. On one level this was fruitless, in that Zhang was ousted yet again in June 1920 by the return of Tan Yankai, but it did bring Mao into contact with articles and comments about the first translations of Karl Marx available in China.

Karl Marx (1818–83).

Mao began (probably accidentally) to frame his articles along more Marxist lines, particularly with regard to women, whose oppressed position he saw as being at the heart of Chinese problems. He was further impressed by the behaviour of the newly formed Communist Russian state, which had unilaterally repealed the unequal treaties enforced by the Western powers on China. He embarked, briefly, on a study of Russian, but struggled with the Cyrillic alphabet.

Meanwhile, experimental anarchist communes were not achieving the success they had hoped for. Mao continued to be active in local Changsha education, setting up a Cultural Book Society in order to encourage his colleagues to embrace the fertile new ideas let in by the May Fourth Movement. Still inspired in part by anarchism, Mao began to support the plan not of an independent China, but of a federation of twenty-seven 'small Chinas', with each province achieving a form of autonomy. His native Hunan, he argued, should be the model:

> For the past four thousand years, Chinese politics has always opted for grand outlines of large-scale projects with big methods. The result has been a country outwardly strong but inwardly weak; solid at the top but ... senseless and corrupt underneath. Since the founding of the Republic, famous people and great men have talked loudly about the constitution, the parliament, the presidential system and the cabinet system. But the more noisily they

> talk, the bigger the mess they make ... We want to narrow the scope and talk about self-rule and self-government in Hunan.[1]

In fact, Hunan was already largely self-governing. With a population of thirty million and a large land area, it had all the attributes of a small state, and Tan Yankai, back as governor for the third time, began making steps to impose a limited form of democracy, in which only the relatively rich would participate in the election of new officials. Mao and his colleagues preferred a form of universal suffrage, with Mao even arguing that children as young as fifteen should have the right to vote. Mao led a public meeting on 8 October 1920, and was one of the three authors of a petition for 'rule by the people' presented to the governor soon afterwards.

Even as Mao was debating sedately, more revolutionarily minded individuals were tearing down the governor's flag. Tan Yankai used this as an excuse to criticise the potential that democracy offered for mob rule, particularly in a place like Hunan where less than 10 per cent of the population could read. As so often seemed to happen in early twentieth-century China, the efforts were for naught anyway, because the governor was soon ousted by a military rival, Zhao Hengti.

Mao's personal circumstances were changing. He was appointed principal of a local primary school which was affiliated with his teacher-training college. He was now financially secure, and risked becoming one of the very bourgeoisie he wanted to overthrow. Also, early in 1920,

Yang Kaihui with Mao's children, Anying and Anqing.

Mao gained his first serious girlfriend, although the pair were separated by autumn, when he began pursuing Yang Kaihui, the daughter of the late Professor Yang.

Mao's disillusionment with the independence movement led him to call for a group dedicated to direct action. In October 1920, he was one of five attendees at the inauguration of a Marxist Study Circle in Hunan. He soon admitted that his interests in anarchism and dreams of an independent Hunan were misguided, and that the best possible chance of achieving lasting change in his China was through the revolutionary methods used by the Russians:

> The Russian method represents a road newly discovered after all the other roads have turned out to be dead ends. Social policy is no method at all, because all it does is patch up some leaks. Social democracy resorts to a parliament ... but in reality the laws passed by a parliament always protect the propertied class. Anarchism rejects all authority, and I fear that such a doctrine can never be realised ... The radical type of communism, or the ideology of the workers and the peasants, which employs the methods of class dictatorship, can be expected to achieve results. Hence it is the best method to use.[2]

Although Mao still wrote progressive essays about the evils of traditional marriage, he was soon prevailed upon to make an honest woman of Kaihui. Their marriage got Kaihui expelled from her missionary school. The couple were married in 1920 and moved into a house on the eastern outskirts of Changsha the following year. Until that point, Mao had let Kaihui sleep in his room at the school, in flagrant contravention of school regulations. Then, as in later life, he ignored rules whenever it suited him. But even as Mao prepared to set up home with his wife, who was soon pregnant with their first child, he was already seeing another woman behind her back.

Mao left for Shanghai in June 1921, and was one of the fifty-three people present on 23 July, at the 'first meeting' of the newly formed Chinese Communist Party. Actually, it was not the first meeting at all, and Mao was something of a latecomer. The Chinese Communist Party had been formed, in secret, a year earlier, and it was only later propaganda which insisted that the 23 July meeting was the first, thereby awarding Mao a place amongst the Party's founder members in propaganda imagery and reportage. The Shanghai meeting also had one Hendricus Sneevliet in attendance, a member of the Russian-backed Communist International (Comintern for short, founded in 1919) whose previous posting had been organising communist activity in Dutch-ruled Indonesia. With him was a 'Mr Nikolsky' from the eastern Russian branch. They were offering funding and 'guidance' for the Chinese Communist Party, but they soon disagreed over the idea that revolution would have to arise from the proletariat – the downtrodden labourers of the industrialised cities – in imitation of the situation in Russia. But China's proletariat was tiny in comparison to its rural peasantry. To the annoyance of the foreign attendees, Mao's fellow Chinese communists argued that revolution in China would need to take a different form from that in Russia.

Russian involvement was eventually tolerated, if only for the $5,000 in funding it brought with it. Mao's first task as a local agent was to increase the size of the Changsha cell to thirty members, which he did without difficulty. He resigned his primary-school principal's job in order to set up a 'Self-Study University' to bring education to the masses; he somehow achieved this with a local government grant, rather than secret money from the Comintern. Perhaps with Comintern guidance, he also began to agitate about working conditions for labourers.

With his teaching background, Mao naturally emphasised education, joining in a loose alliance with the Young Men's Christian Association (YMCA) to set up night schools, while secretly ensuring that many of the teachers were Party members, and that the textbook used to teach reading skills contained many socialist ideas. Others were more direct in their action. A Hunan Workingmen's Association briefly flourished, only to have its two ringleaders executed by Hunan's governor Zhao Hengti for inciting a strike at a local cotton mill. Zhao defended himself with the claim that they had been plotting revolution, denying that he had any complaint with labourers' associations.

Meanwhile, the Shanghai headquarters of the Chinese communists called for members to work particularly hard at courting the railway workers. The railways were vital transport conduits and, unlike rivers, required heavy investment of capital.

On 9 September 1922, railwaymen blocked the line at Yuezhou, north of Changsha, protesting over their working conditions. Governor Zhao did not interfere, since the area was under the jurisdiction of a rival warlord, whose men killed six protesters. For Mao, however, the result was the same: oppressors had stifled righteous rebellion. 'Fellow workers of the labour groups!' he wrote. 'Such dark, tyrannical and cruel oppression is visited only on our labouring class. How angry should we be? How bitterly must we hate? How forcefully should we rise up? Take revenge! Fellow workers of the whole country, arise and struggle against the enemy!'[3]

Until this point, Mao's influence was peripheral. His writings and articles supported revolution, but he was far away from the physical conflict. His agitations, however, were starting to bear fruit. A miners' strike in nearby Anyuan on 13 September 1922 was a great success for the workers, resulting in significantly better pay conditions, working arrangements, and holidays. Elsewhere, railwaymen threatened a national rail strike, and won a wage increase.

Mao was also instrumental in the formation of a Changsha Masons' and Carpenters' Union, an organisation of workers dissatisfied with the failure of their more traditional trading guild to win better conditions for them. By October 1922, following a magistrate's refusal to approve a pay rise, the leaders were meeting at Mao's Clearwater Pond home to arrange a strike. For the first time, Mao was at the forefront of the action, leading the picketing workers in songs and the chanting of slogans to keep up their spirits, and acting as their spokesman with the governor's officers, who tried to intimidate the workers with threats of violence.

Mao's strike efforts gained the union the 50 per cent pay rise that the traditional guilds had failed to secure through negotiations and banquets. It was a ringing endorsement of his policies, but also showed where his allegiances lay. While Mao was fighting for workers' rights in intense meetings, his wife gave birth to his first son in his absence; it was a significant indicator of Mao's priorities.

Further government clampdowns, most notably the 7 February Massacre of 1923 that resulted in around forty deaths, demonstrated that protests alone would not be enough to topple the government. Mao began to believe that Russian military aid would be required. His successes as a protestor and negotiator gained the approval of his Communist associates, and he became one of the nine members of the Central Committee of the Communist Party. However, he was soon forced to maintain a dual role by taking part in an attempt to combine Communist aims with those of Sun Yat-sen's Nationalists. Like many other Communists, Mao also joined the Nationalists, hoping to pursue revolutionary aims from within. After the early successes of 1922, many of Mao's Communist colleagues were swamped or converted by their association with the Nationalists, and party activity seemed to stagnate. Mao, however, remained an ardent revolutionary.

Sun Yat-sen died in March 1925, leading to an internal Nationalist power struggle in which Mao seemed to want no part. By December 1925, Mao headed home with his wife and in-laws, claiming (perhaps with reason) to be ill and exhausted, but also disillusioned with the slow progress and with what he saw as Nationalist unwillingness to pursue true reform. However, Mao's convalescence only lasted a few months. On 30 May 1926, Japanese troops in Shanghai shot strikers at a textile mill. Protests sprang up all over China, leading to further attacks on foreigners, and killings by Japanese and British troops attempting to disperse crowds.

Mao's return to his birthplace, combined with his dissatisfaction with the urban politics of the Russian-influenced communists, led him to place an increased value on the participation of peasants in the countryside. Temporarily, he all but gave up on the Communists, instead dedicating himself to the left wing of the Nationalists. He went to Guangzhou in south China, where he set up the *Political Weekly*, a journal designed to counteract the Nationalist right wing. Mao cunningly spoke to the Nationalists as if he were one of them, and not as a Communist: 'Uniting with Russia and accepting communists are important tactics of our party,' he told his Nationalist associates, 'in pursuing the goal of victory in the revolution.'[4]

Not everyone was fooled. In the power vacuum left by the death of Sun Yat-sen, one of the Nationalists' new leaders was Chiang Kai-shek. The son of a relatively wealthy family, Chiang was one of the first Chinese to receive a modern military education, part of which he received in Japan. He was Sun Yat-sen's brother-in-law, but it was his control of the Nationalist army that made him Sun's de facto heir. Like Sun before him, Chiang was what Mao called a bourgeois revolutionary, only interested in changing the rulers at the top of China's government, and not 'liberating' the peasants. Chiang did not like the increasing emphasis on the needs of the workers, nor did he appreciate Mao's statements that anyone who did not want to overthrow all landlords and destroy the notion of private property was an enemy of the people. For Chiang, however, the last straw was the arrival of yet another Russian adviser, who questioned Chiang's strategy in retaking north China from the warlords.

By the dawn of 1926, Chiang had resigned over this

Chiang Kai-shek with Wang Jingwei.

attempted Russian interference in what he thought to be a local matter. He believed, perhaps with justification, that the Russians and Communist sympathisers were planning a takeover of the Nationalist party and, as one of their most outspoken critics, he could expect to be a casualty. He feared being kidnapped and dragged off to Moscow where he would be unable to fight back. And so, on 20 March, Chiang made a pre-emptive strike. He declared martial law, arrested all Communists in the Guangzhou area, and put the Russian advisers under armed guard. It was a bloodless coup, with no reported deaths – a surgical removal of Chiang's political enemies before they could make their move. The Russians were packed off home, and Chiang's chief Chinese rival, Wang Jingwei, was sent to Europe on extended leave.

By April, the suspicious Nationalists were establishing ground rules for involvement with the Communists. Since the organisations had common goals, the Communists' presence was tolerated, but their number and role were limited: no Communist could lead a department in the Nationalist government, and Communists could not make up more than a third of any government committee. The Nationalists hoped that this would ensure that all decisions favoured themselves rather than their underhand revolutionary associates.

While the Nationalist Party's army under Chiang went on to bring all of south China under KMT rule, Mao returned to Hunan via Shanghai. There, the Communist Party appointed him as the leader of its Peasant Movement Committee, charged with ensuring that the revolution was brought to the countryside, and that this happened in the name of the Communists, not the Nationalists.

The Nationalists had troubles of their own, splitting

into two rival camps in late 1926, with Chiang's supporters claiming that the new capital was in Nanchang, while his left-leaning rivals, including Sun Yat-sen's widow, announced that the capital was with them in Wuhan. Mao made his way to Wuhan, where the Communists hoped to convince the left-wing Nationalists that they had nothing to fear from them, and thereby win some concessions. *En route*, he travelled for a month among peasants during a Chinese winter, and reported that uprisings were fomenting all over the country. His comments on the coming troubles in the countryside, and how it might affect some of the richer allies of the Nationalists, made for chilling reading.

'The main targets of their attacks are the local bullies, the evil gentry and the lawless landlords,' he wrote, 'but in passing they hit out against patriarchal ideas and institutions of all kinds.' In overthrowing symbols of the old order, this was already within the general aims of the Nationalists, but Mao also enthusiastically alluded to a new class of bullies, whose rule seemed just as arbitrary and unpleasant. 'The peasant associations have now become the sole organs of authority ... Even trifles such as a quarrel between husband and wife are brought before the peasant association. The association actually dictates all rural affairs.' Mao saw this is as a good thing. After all, the dictatorship of the formerly oppressed was one of the aims of Communism. Mao's report argued that the end (Communist utopia) would justify the means (brutal uprising).

'This is what ordinary people call "going too far",' he wrote. 'A revolution is not like inviting people to dinner, or writing an essay or painting a picture, or doing embroidery; it cannot be so refined, so leisurely and so gentle ... A revolution is an uprising, an act of violence ... If the peasants do not use extremely great force, they cannot possibly overthrow the deeply rooted powers of the landlords ... To put it bluntly, it is necessary to bring about a brief reign of terror in every rural area.'[5]

Mao called for the execution of prominent landlords or oppressive gentry in every region, believing that a few conspicuous deaths would bring others into line – killing a chicken, as a Chinese proverb went, in order to scare the monkeys. He viewed the peasant rebels as pure heroes, casting aside all that was wrong, which for Mao meant gambling (except for gambling on a successful Communist reform), opium addiction, religion (except for belief in the power of the Communist Party), and secret societies (except for the Communist Party, which was the biggest secret society of all). Some within the Communist Party tried to suppress Mao's report, but unexpurgated copies of it were soon in circulation. Meanwhile, workers anticipating the arrival of Chiang Kai-shek's Nationalist army in Shanghai went on strike. But Chiang did not attack the city, and the uprising was brutally suppressed by the garrison commander, who executed the strikers.

The Communists and Nationalists were back where they had started, with each rightly suspecting that the other was only a fair-weather friend. Once Shanghai was under his control, Chiang organised an attack on the Communists. Mao's associate Zhou Enlai called a general strike, but

Nationalist troops shot into an unarmed crowd including women and children. Several hundred died on 27 April, but for the Communists, the worst was yet to come.

Maoism

During the month following Chiang's betrayal in Shanghai, the Communist Party lost 50,000 members. Determined to eradicate the Communists, Nationalist troops in Changsha rounded up and shot all sympathisers and suspected sympathisers. In the countryside, peasant collectives either stood their ground with sharpened bamboo sticks against gun-wielding Nationalists, or pre-empted disaster by dissolving their Communist-influenced village committees. The latter action often proved as dangerous as the former, since it allowed surviving local landowners to lead a backlash against them.

The eventual death toll in four Hunan counties was 300,000, a number of significant concern to the Communists and the subject of heated debates among the Russians, who were at least partly responsible for goading the Nationalists into action. It obviously ended the united front between the two parties. Regardless of their shared interests in overthrowing the warlords, neither would ever fully trust the other again. Prominent Communists went into hiding.

With the cities largely in the hands of the Nationalists, Mao's interest in fostering a peasant military force gained new attractiveness – it was, after all, probably the only remaining option. His superiors in the remnants of the Communist organisation agreed, at a secret party

Soldiers of the Nationalist Army prepare to leave for Nanjing, 1927.

conference in Hankou on 7 August 1927, that the Communists would have to act more like a secret society than a political party.

Mao was once more a committee member in the reorganised Communist Party, but not with much power. He appeared to have already made enemies within the party, with a stubborn attitude that paid off on a picket line, but not in meetings with his supposed comrades-in-arms. He had achieved great successes, it was true, in Hunan, but there he was a local boy. Some of his colleagues tried to have him moved to Shanghai or Sichuan, where he would have had to build up his contacts from scratch.

Nevertheless, for now Mao held onto Hunan, and was duly dispatched there to organise the local part of an uprising the Communists planned for the time of the autumn harvest. Although he cannot have realised it at the time, his period quite literally in the wilderness would last for twenty-two more years.

While his superiors were still discussing the best course of action to take, Mao had already ditched the Nationalist flag in favour of the Communists' red banner. This was probably more necessary in Hunan than any other place, since locals would be unlikely to flock to the standard of the army that had recently killed so many of their neighbours. He also summarised his stance on military action with what would become one of his most famous quotations, in which he outlined that every one of the Communists' enemies had used force, and that it was time for them to do so in similar measure. 'From now on we should pay the greatest attention to military affairs,' he wrote. 'We must know that political power is obtained out of the barrel of a gun.'[1]

Deep down, his comments contained the seed of a more sinister form of Communism than Mao had previously espoused. His comrades believed that revolution would only come when the people *chose* to rise up. Mao's calling for military force beforehand, it could be argued, simply turned the Communists into another band of would-be warlords. His plans did not go down well with his superiors, leading to a hurried exchange of argumentative letters in which they accused him of slacking in his duty to organise a true rebellion, and placing unwise reliance on the arrival of military assistance that the Party was unable to guarantee.

Mao deliberately ignored Party plans, which overestimated his available forces. At the time of the uprising, he had barely a thousand former Nationalist troops, a handful of out-of-work miners, and a few of the surviving peasant militia from the countryside. It was not much, but he called it the First Workers' and Peasants' Revolutionary Army.

But the plans for the uprising were already known to the authorities, and as Mao and his forces made their final preparations, they were captured by a group of mercenaries working for the Nationalists. As a ringleader, Mao was to be taken to the headquarters and executed. He was almost successful in bribing them to release him, but his plans were thwarted by one of the higher officers. Only a couple of hundred yards away from the place of execution, Mao made a run for it, scurrying into thick bushes on the far side of a nearby pond, and keeping as still as possible. 'The soldiers pursued me,' he recounted, 'and forced some peasants to help them search. Many times they came very near, once or twice so close that I could almost have touched them, but somehow I escaped discovery, although half-a-dozen times I gave up hope, feeling certain I would be recaptured.'[2]

He hid until the search parties dispersed in the evening, and then made a night dash across the mountain. By the time Mao was out of danger, the uprising was over. The crucial military element had been defeated, not by Nationalist strategy, but by another group of local militia, little better than bandits, who wanted to steal the Communists' superior weapons. Without troops, Mao urged the Party to call off the lesser peasant uprising (which would have met with unmitigated disaster) and the revolt was over before it could truly begin.

Similar setbacks ruined the chances of other Communist cells across south China. In November, the surviving ringleaders met in Shanghai and agreed that although their plans had been sound, the missing piece was still the involvement of the peasantry – not merely their participation in the fighting, but also the silent support needed in order to avoid betrayals. The Comintern, dissatisfied with the lack of results, sent Besso Lominadze, a young Russian 'adviser' with little appreciation of the Chinese situation. Lominadze wasted little time in calling for the dismissal of Party members whose revolutionary fervour he regarded as below par. Mao held onto his central committee membership, but was sacked from one of his posts.

Mao seemed undeterred by his punishment. The Chinese Communist revolution often had four contradictory policies: those of its supposed headquarters in Russia, of the Chinese headquarters in Shanghai, of the local Party organisations, and of the peasants on the ground. Believing that only the last of these would actually achieve anything, Mao returned to the countryside and the remnants of the peasant militias.

While Mao licked his wounds in the countryside, the faction of foreign advisers backed a disastrous revolt in southern China. Zhang Tailei, a leading young Communist, returned to the south from Shanghai with instructions to lead an uprising in the provincial capital, Guangzhou (Canton).

Zhang Tailei's statue in Guangzhou shows him wounded and reaching for his gun.

His German adviser insisted that the time was right, despite protests from commanders that sympathetic local troops were outgunned and outnumbered. With the benefit of surprise, the communists swiftly seized key points in the city, and Zhang Tailei proclaimed the commencement of a 'Canton Soviet' or a 'Guangzhou Commune' – sources disagree on the best translation. His new utopia lasted for less than three days before it was crushed by the arrival of government reinforcements. Several hundred people died during the fighting – some six *thousand* were massacred in the aftermath of the government's return to power.[3]

Many of the would-be rebels of the Canton Soviet lost their lives, including Zhang Tailei, who was shot in an ambush as he returned from a meeting. Like Mao, Zhang had been a staunch advocate of the need to pursue a different sort of Communism in China – not an appeal to the urban workers as in Russia, but an appeal to the peasants of the countryside. He had gamely tried to initiate a labourers' strike in Guangzhou, but seemed to have been pre-empted by his military allies jumping the gun – it was suggested in later Party conferences that they had done so deliberately in order to make the Canton Soviet coincide with a communist conference in Russia. Zhang's last message to the Comintern, sent three days before the uprising, displays a certain optimistic, even religious trust in good fortune:

> Our strength is not great, but we believe that once [the] uprising is launched, it will for sure receive the help of the masses. A common people's revolutionary movement like this will for sure influence the enemy's forces, and cause their dissolution. If we can hold on for two weeks, we will for sure receive concrete help internationally.[4]

On the eve of the uprising, he addressed a room full of revolutionaries with a similar fervour, saying: 'Comrades, tonight we put an end to the old history. Tonight, we conquer the last icy mountain on our path forward.'[5]

Described by Zhang himself as the 'high tide' of months of agitation and demonstration in Guangzhou, the uprising was a catalogue of mistakes. The Communists captured several artillery pieces, but only one of their number knew how to operate them. They took sixty prisoners from the government forces, but could not agree on what to do with them. Eventually, the enemies seized control of the revolutionary headquarters and executed their captors.[6] Although every previous uprising and strike thus far had eventually failed, Zhang turned out to have no plan for retreat. After his death, his underlings realised they did not know how to evade the onrushing counterattack.[7]

Back at the Party headquarters, there was much finger-pointing and hand-wringing about who was to blame. Even as the Canton Soviet rose and fell, and the workers of Guangzhou paid the price in savage government reprisals, the central committee was drafting rebukes to Mao, accusing him of straying from Party doctrine and disobeying orders. But Mao, and several other dissenters, had managed what the urban agents had not – they had formed local, countryside clusters of communist sympathisers. The central committee might regard them as the *wrong sort of revolutionary*, but that was hardly the point.

Mao claimed himself to be the leader of the 1st Regiment, 1st Division of the First Workers' and Peasants'

The cenotaph at the Guangzhou Martyrs' Park shows rebels with guns, clubs, and cleavers.

Revolutionary Army. He did not mention at the time that there was no second regiment, division, or army. More characteristically for him, he insisted that only volunteers should stay. Anyone who wanted to go home was welcome to do so, although Mao promised that the force would henceforth be organised on properly Communist lines: each unit would have a committee to arbitrate disputes, and the officers would not be permitted to beat their men. Meanwhile, the men were under strict instructions to recognise that their most important allies were the very peasants through whose fields they would be marching. They were to treat them with heightened respect and pay for anything they took. Mao reasonably hoped that such an attitude would be a propaganda coup, and do more than any victory to ensure the local population would realise that *this* army was different, and was truly working in their interests.

Mao's policy was soon put to the test, as the newly

formed all-volunteer army headed for the high ground. For the next year, Mao's First Army hid out in Jinggang, a mountain range on the Hunan–Jiangxi border. Militarily, it was a risky decision, since there was little food, and Mao's soldiers had to be supplied by grain delivered on foot by porters. This, however, would only present a problem if the Nationalists were able to cut off his supplies, and he enjoyed support from the fields below, courtesy of his policy of fair treatment.

Through late 1927 and early 1928, Mao's roving army made several abortive attempts to set up 'Workers', Peasants', and Soldiers' Soviet Governments' in the local area, defeated only by incursions from the Nationalists. In each new village, Mao and his militia would encourage the locals to turn on their landlords, thereby wiping out their debts and 'freeing' them to return to work as common owners of the land. A feature of Mao's methods was his *lack* of involvement. Instead of marching in and targeting his victims in approved Party style, he would leave the peasants to do the killing themselves, making them complicit in the revolution, but also murderers in the eyes of any Nationalist forces should the village be retaken. Mao's definition of what constituted an evil oppressor depended largely on how much money he needed. 'If the masses don't understand what "landed tyrants" means,' he wrote, 'you can tell them it means the moneyed or "the rich"'.[8] In some places, this could mean a farm that had chickens in the yard.

Mao also worked on recruiting other leaders to his cause, donating rifles to rag-tag militias and offering to send

Communist instructors to 'help' them organise their forces. By February 1928, Mao had his 2nd Regiment, built from the combined forces of two local leaders.

The first major test for Mao's reorganised peasant forces came on 17 February, when a Nationalist battalion occupied a town close to his base. An assault on them might have seemed foolhardy, but the increased Nationalist presence so close to Mao's food supply might otherwise have defeated him without a shot being fired.

Mao attacked the Nationalists as they began their dawn exercises. Most of his opponents were in their underwear and far from their weapons, but some were not caught off-guard, and the fighting went on for some time. Eventually, however, the Nationalist leaders were killed, and the victorious Communists led 100 prisoners back to their nearby base.

Instead of being executed, as they might have expected, the prisoners were set free. Mao told them that they were not the enemy. If they wanted to return home, they were welcome to do so. Otherwise, they could switch sides and join the Communists, who were fighting the *true* enemy. With little to gain from returning to their Nationalist masters, many of the defeated soldiers stayed, swelling the Communist ranks.

Despite such early successes, Mao's behaviour did not make him popular with the Party HQ. Although some lauded Mao's achievements, the head of the Military Committee, Zhou Enlai, was scandalised. It was not enough, he said, that Mao was winning battles against opponents seemingly selected at random; Zhou wanted to see military operations against agreed targets. Perhaps without full grasp of the facts, but more likely parroting the unrealistic aims of the Russian advisers foisted on him by the Comintern, Zhou wrote off Mao as a military opportunist. Zhou could not see the point in coordinating separate militia forces for an operation with a mere 'bandit character', deriding it as a 'plot masquerading as a plan.'

A series of unfortunate deaths and arrests had put a number of inexperienced or incompetent Party officials in positions of power, and in early 1928 a messenger informed Mao that he had been fired from the Hunan provincial committee (which was true) and expelled from the Communist Party (which was not).

Mao was ordered to lend support to another army, that of Zhu De, who had marched up from the far south with defectors from the Nationalists' Fourth Army. Mao did so with some reluctance, eventually uniting his own force with that of Zhu to form a body known locally as the Zhu–Mao Army. It was also called the Fourth Workers' and Peasants' Revolutionary Army, taking its name from Zhu's former loyalties, and soon after its name was changed again to the Fourth Red Army.

Zhu De came from a farming background in China's western province of Sichuan. He was one of the last generation to win a traditional Confucian degree, but also became an opium addict. He fought in the 1911 republican revolution, broke his drug habit in Shanghai in the 1920s, and went to Germany, where he joined the Chinese Communist

Party. He returned to take up a military commission with the Nationalists (as a Communist sympathiser) until, forced to choose, he sided with the Communists. He would eventually become the commander-in-chief of the Red Army, and later, although he retired in 1949, the Chinese head of state.

Although Mao and Zhu were jointly in charge of some 8,000 soldiers, some with significant military experience but others mere peasant militia, Mao was sceptical about their chances. Already, the Communist forces had faced several near-defeats, and while they had growing support in isolated villages, they were still surrounded by enemies. Nor were local people keen to join the Red Army; although they broadly supported its aims, they also wanted to be left alone to farm. With the arrival of a Red Army brigade in a town and the overthrow of local landlords, peasants simply wished to return their fields. It was against Mao's official policy to forcibly conscript anyone into the Red Army, but he hoped that his men would continue to enjoy local support.

In May 1928, Mao and Zhu issued a simple poem to the men, designed to summarise their policy on engaging their enemies. They proposed a war of attrition, avoiding direct conflict, and never engaging the enemy directly: a guerrilla strategy heavily redolent of passages from Sun Tzu's *Art of War*:

The enemy advances, I withdraw
The enemy rests, I harass

The enemy tires, I attack
The enemy withdraws, I pursue.[9]

The soldiers were also issued with Six Main Points for Attention, which updated Mao's original plea for them to treat local people well, and the deceptively simple Three Main Rules of Discipline: obey orders, do not steal, hand in anything confiscated from enemies. At the time, these ideas were unpopular with many Party members, but others were coming around to Mao's approach.

Many of Mao's associates had 'revolutionary companions' – bedmates while they were far away from their wives. In 1928 Mao began co-habiting with an eighteen-year-old local girl called He Zizhen. Zizhen had the kind of education that would appeal to Mao, with a traditional scholar for a father and a more modern education courtesy of a Finnish missionary. She would ultimately become Mao's third wife, following the death of his second, and would bear him several children.

In June 1928, Mao's superiors met in the Sixth Party Congress of the Chinese Communists, held in Russia. There, they agreed that China was still far from true revolution, and that it would be a long struggle to turn most Chinese into people who might support and participate in revolt for themselves. They were, step by step, acknowledging that Mao's strategy seemed likely to reap greater benefits in the long term.

But Mao's advance was not without its setbacks. In late 1928, the Zhu–Mao army was split and suffered several defeats as a result of interference from Party higher-ups who refused to play Mao's waiting game. They entered into direct conflict with several Nationalist regiments and were forced to retreat in most instances, their one 'victory' being a holding action at a narrow mountain pass that levelled many of the differences between the opposing armies.

Their losses showed that the best way to run forces in the region was from a command post close at hand. Mao was elated to receive a Party communication in November that made him the Secretary of a 'Front Committee' – effectively acknowledging that he was already in charge of local decision-making.

With winter approaching, Mao's army faced intense supply problems. With so many men in such a poorly resourced area, inflation made everyday necessities hard to find. Concerned that harsher conditions over the cold months would lose him many of his less committed soldiers, Mao tried to reform his payment systems. There would be no more wages. Instead, soldiers were paid in the supplies that they required – but those supplies still needed to come from somewhere.

In a sense, Mao's army's most precious commodity was its class enemies, since its chief means of acquiring money came from overthrowing local 'landlords and bullies'. But with all the local landlords and bullies executed or imprisoned, the Red Army had to range ever further in search of class enemies to overthrow. In some cases, the 'property' seized by Mao's troops was an illegal crop of opium, the conversion of which into cash would turn them into drug smugglers. When not even opium was forthcoming, Mao turned to methods of extortion little different from those of the warlords he claimed to oppose.

Foreshadowing the bitter ironies of Mao's later years, his signature appears on a 'fundraising letter' from the period that demands donations from local shopkeepers, and threatens violence if they do not volunteer it: 'because of the current shortage of food supplies, we are writing to you now to request that you kindly collect on our behalf 5,000 dollars, 7,000 pairs of straw sandals and 7,000 pairs of socks, [and] 300 bolts of white cloth ... If you ignore our requests, it will be proof that [you] merchants are collaborating with the reactionaries ... In that case we will be obliged to burn down all the reactionary shops in [the town].'[10] Issuing such letters was a last-ditch measure. Once Mao did it, he knew it was time to move his troops to another area before they exhausted any remaining local support.

Then, in December 1928, in the depths of Hunan's bitter winter, one Peng Dehuai arrived at the head of 800 defecting Nationalists, with news that thousands of hostile Nationalist troops were approaching Mao's base.

The Long March

One of the Chinese Communist Party's greatest military leaders, Peng Dehuai began as a professional soldier with the Nationalists, before being purged for his left-wing views and turning to the Communists. He was destined to become the second-in-command of Mao's forces and ultimately the leader of the Chinese army.

The First Committee agreed that the mountain base would be evacuated in two waves. First, Mao and Zhu would sneak away with the bulk of the forces. Peng's small detachment would hold the passes until the Zhu–Mao forces could cause a diversion far enough away to distract the soldiers attacking Peng. Then, Peng would also make his getaway, along with the less mobile residents: women, children, and the injured.

Mao let his ally down. On the night of 14 January 1929, Mao's forces captured a Nationalist detachment and feasted heartily on their food. But the following day, they kept running, without any thought of turning back for the agreed diversion. Peng held his positions for another week, before making a desperate bid for safety. He lost two-thirds of his soldiers, and most of the wounded and sick.

Mao experienced setbacks of his own, along with the realisation that, without their mountain base, the Communists would now have to remain permanently on the move. In the spring, he also became a father again, when

He Zizhen gave birth to a daughter. There was no place for infants in the Red Army, and the nameless girl was handed over to a peasant family that same day, her fate unknown.[1]

Communication with Party headquarters and other Communist cells was now sporadic at best. When orders did arrive from Zhou Enlai, they unhelpfully suggested that Mao return to Shanghai, scattering his surviving platoons undercover across the entire area to wait for the coast to become clear, while preaching revolutionary ideas.

Arguments over the next step continued for several months, until the establishment of a new committee to oversee the Fourth Army forced Mao's hand. He threatened to resign and was eventually corralled into an inferior position as Party representative, with the lead post of Secretary now in the hands of Chen Yi, a fellow leader with whom Mao had a series of blazing rows. However, what at first seemed to be a demotion for Mao forced him to use the only weapon available: the terminology of the Communist Party itself. When faced with criticism from others, Mao would question whether such criticism was justified, or a sign that his critic had failed to comprehend Party doctrine.

Mao was able to trade on his role as a Party representative, couching his opposition to Chen Yi in terms of the latter's lack of loyalty to higher ideals. While their superiors back in Shanghai tried to resolve the dispute, Mao went into retreat, claiming ill health, and occupying himself reading books in a secluded mountain residence.

He was eventually ordered to attend an Army Congress.

He did so with great reluctance, arriving on a stretcher to emphasise his sickness. Mao and his colleagues were ordered to stop antagonising each other, but Mao still somehow secured a personal victory. He spent several months in the hills of Fujian, ignoring two requests to return to his duties. He only consented to return to action after receiving letters from Zhu De, Chen Yi, and the entire Front Committee acknowledging that they needed him.

Mao returned on the understanding that he would work out his problems with his colleagues. Instead, he attacked them, codifying in Party reports the idea that those of a military background must realise that their Party loyalties needed to come first. He also laid into insubordination, decrying the 'ultrademocracy' that allowed anyone faced with an unwelcome order to refuse it and pass their refusal off as a revolutionary achievement. Although Mao may have been somewhat contradictory in attacking both blind obedience to superiors' orders *and* the questioning of such orders, he had his motives. Mao's reports established that only he, as Party representative, had the final say on what constituted loyalty, a dangerous grey area that would characterise the absolute power he wielded in later life.

Soon, more by luck than judgement, Mao found his Party position further reinforced. The catalyst, again, was a railway – this time the Chinese Eastern Railway, a Russian line that crossed over Chinese territory. The Chinese Eastern Railway was built by the Russians in the late nineteenth century, shortening the long journey from Europe to Russia's far-eastern port of Vladivostok. In 1924, Russia's new Soviet government had officially renounced all claims in the region, *except* for the railway.

Chiang Kai-shek's Nationalist government pressured Moscow to hand the railway over to them, but the Russians fought back. Moscow planned to send a few soldiers over the border into Manchuria on a brief raid, but also sent word to Communist allies to increase their activities in both Manchuria and the area in which Mao's forces were located. The railway argument blew over long before news of these plans reached the Chinese Communists, but the scheming was taken to be a tacit Russian endorsement of Mao's behaviour.

A new General Front Committee was formed, designed to control all local Communist forces. Mao was made Secretary, thereby putting him in charge of the people who now commanded his Fourth Army, among others. It was a promotion designed to save face all round – a recognition that Mao the rule-breaker had somehow proved more successful than his critics.

However, Mao's problems with headquarters were still not over. His new nemesis was Li Lisan, another well-travelled Party official who disliked his emphasis on the rural revolution. A native of Hunan, Li had joined the Chinese Communist Party while in Paris. Back in China, he rose to prominence at Party headquarters, and clung to the same desire for an urban workers' revolution as espoused by Zhou Enlai. Li still insisted on activities close to urban centres, which Mao felt placed his soldiers in unnecessary jeopardy. In July 1930, Peng Dehuai occupied Changsha for nine days, scoring a hefty propaganda coup, but evacuating ahead of retaliatory troops. On 1 August 1930, Li ordered an action in Nanchang to mark the anniversary of an earlier uprising in 1927. Some of Mao's militia fired shots in the air near the railway station on the outskirts, and then ran back into hiding.

Li's plan, however, did score some victories. Mao launched a reluctant strike against the town of Ji'an. Although he made several attempts to withdraw, the town's Nationalist defenders were unaware of his disinterest in pursuing the attack. Perhaps spooked by news of other Communist troop movements, perhaps fearing for their own supplies, the Nationalists secretly withdrew, and Mao occupied the town without a fight. His men were able to occupy the town for six weeks, before fleeing ahead of a relief force.

Even as Mao took Ji'an, Li's days were numbered. The Communist Party's Russian advisers had smuggled a radio transmitter into China, rendering communications with Moscow instantaneous. Supporting peasant revolution was now a mandatory part of Communist policy, and Li was unable to pretend that communication lines were too long to allow debate. In November, Li was recalled to Moscow in disgrace.

In the aftermath of Changsha, Nationalist reprisals got personal. Any known associates of recognised Communist ringleaders were rounded up and killed. Mao used the pseudonym Li Desheng, but was too conspicuously known by his real name to save his relatives. The graves of Mao's parents were dug up by Nationalist soldiers – the ultimate insult. Nor were the living spared. The abandoned Yang Kaihui was executed outside the city gates.[2] Her three children were taken into hiding, although the youngest, Anlong, died of dysentery in Shanghai early the next year.

Next, rashly, Chiang Kai-shek promised his council that he would eradicate Mao's Communists before the following summer. But Mao's army had grown significantly. It now numbered around 40,000 and, while still primitively armed, had benefited greatly from its policy of welcoming Nationalist defectors. It also enjoyed a reputation as being a purely volunteer force, although in truth it was plagued with desertions, which Mao policed with his customary lethal force. Most soldiers now had rifles, largely stolen from the Nationalists, and Mao had imposed some basic recruitment criteria – he could afford to turn away the old, the sick, and the infirm. However, more advanced military technology was still sparse. Mao's army lacked artillery, or great numbers of mortars and machine guns. They also lacked good field communications. Headquarters might be able to talk direct to Moscow by radio, but units in the countryside still had to rely largely on messengers travelling on foot.

This slowness of communications led to many misunderstandings. For instance, a man arrived in January 1931 to relieve Mao of a post he did not even know he had held: Acting Secretary of the Central Bureau. Mao and his 'replacement' shared uneasy control of the army for two months, before news arrived from Shanghai of Li Lisan's fall from power the previous November. This meant that Mao's 'replacement', a Li appointee, was discredited, and Mao was officially back in charge, although in actual fact, he had never actually stepped down in the first place. He assumed sole command of his army again, with no way of knowing whether or not the new situation was just about to be countermanded by another decision that would similarly have taken several weeks to reach him. Under such unstable conditions, it is perhaps no surprise that the army gravitated to the leader they knew.

Mao called these foreign appointees the 'Returned Students' – credentialled interlopers coming back from overseas junkets, whose qualifications and linguistic abilities threatened to marginalise him. There was no love lost between them; one snide critic dismissed Mao as 'muddy-legs', as if he were a clueless hick, fresh off the rice paddies, with no understanding about the bigger picture.[3]

Facing such rivalry, Mao clung to his limited strengths. Classical ideas were out, since they were connected with the old order, although Mao continued to make classical allusions as a form of homespun wisdom, or as in the case of his military poetry, to lift ideas from classical authors and pass them off as his own work. Instead, he emphasised that only someone with direct experience of an issue was qualified to speak on it – alluding, of course, to his own grassroots situation when compared to that of the distant HQ. 'If you have not investigated a certain problem, you will lose your right to speak on it', he wrote. 'There are also people who say: "Show me where it is written in a book" ...

This book-worshipping method of conducting research [is] dangerous.'[4]

While such petty politics muddied the waters, Mao's army was forced to dodge several campaigns by Chiang Kai-shek's forces. He had already avoided defeat in Chiang's first attempt to cut him off, evading one army and surprising another, stealing further equipment and gaining more defectors. The spring saw a renewed Nationalist attack, with 200,000 men. Mao's troops followed his strategy of ambushes and withdrawals, only engaging the enemy when sure of victory. He achieved five victories in a row by May, acquiring significant new supplies of men and materiel.

This accomplishment secured the reputations of Mao and his colleagues as military leaders with whom headquarters should not trifle, and led to massive propaganda successes for the Communists. It also placed Chiang Kai-shek in an embarrassing position. He could no longer claim that the Communists were a minor irritation he could deal with when he felt like it. Stung into action, Chiang personally led a further 300,000 troops into the south, in a third encirclement campaign designed to wipe Mao out.

The Red Army began with a repeat of its former tactics, running for the south, hoping to lure the Nationalists into pursuit, ready for a surprise attack at an undetermined future date. All the while, they continued to pester their pursuers, firing guns at night to deprive the Nationalists of sleep, and seeding their path with traps. The Red Army was eventually able to claim a 'victory' in the region, both through the measures it took to escape and the simple fact that Chiang's campaign to eradicate it was a failure. Mao had also been inadvertently helped by the arrival of two other groups, whose appearance had forced Chiang to change his plans.

In Guangdong, just to Hunan's south, the ousted Nationalist Wang Jingwei proclaimed a new, independent government encompassing several provinces – a direct challenge to the southern regime that Chiang Kai-shek was claiming to run from Nanjing in the east. One of the first acts of Wang's new government was to invade the crucial region of Hunan. Chiang Kai-shek's troops were forced to meet the invading army and, eventually, to retreat before it. Any plans Chiang may have had for a counter-offensive had to be called off in September, when Japanese forces took Manchuria. Chiang Kai-shek pulled out of Hunan, both to avoid the southern armies and to fight the Japanese, Wang's invaders melted away, and since they were the last men standing, the Communists were able to claim a victory of sorts.

They celebrated by proclaiming the Chinese Soviet Republic in twenty contiguous counties, centring on the town of Ruijin, on 7 November 1931: the anniversary of the Russian Revolution. Mao used the day as an opportunity to announce that the Communists were not merely a force opposed to Chiang Kai-shek, but a legitimate government in waiting:

> From now on, there are two totally different states in the territory of China, one is the so-called Republic

> of China, which is a tool of imperialism ... The other is the Chinese Soviet Republic, the state of the broad masses of exploited and oppressed workers, peasants, soldiers and toilers. Its banner is that of overthrowing imperialism; eliminating the landlord class; bringing down the [Nationalist] warlord government ... and striving for genuine peace and unification of the whole country.[5]

Mao's rhetoric hid more politicking behind the scenes. The original Front Committee had been abolished, and Mao had been 'promoted' to the honorary position of Chairman, or head of the new government, separating him from the army that supplied so much of his power. His suggestion at a meeting that the Japanese invasion would unify most Chinese against a new foe, and should be exploited, fell on deaf ears. Consequently, Mao went into one of his periodic phases of illness, claiming to be too sick to work, and retiring to convalesce. His illness miraculously lifted in March 1932, when news arrived that the army, under Peng Dehuai, had met with disaster by breaking with Mao's previous policy and directly attacking a city. Officially, Peng was still in charge of what was now called the Third Army Group, but Mao was present as an 'adviser' to the First Army, now led by the twenty-five-year-old Lin Biao.

A native of Hubei province, Lin Biao had become a socialist in 1925, and trained as a soldier in Guangdong's Whampoa Military Academy under Chiang Kai-shek. During Chiang's Northern Expedition, Lin had risen through the ranks to battalion commander, but defected to the Communists when Chiang turned on them. Enjoying a reputation as a man who had never lost a battle, Lin Biao remained in action, drilling soldiers or recovering from wounds for the next twenty years.

The conflict between soldiers and distant Party officials continued to cause tension. To these officials, Mao's behaviour still seemed overly cautious, his objectives all but random, his insubordination legendary. Given a choice between following HQ's orders and marching north, or picking off more towns to the west, Mao went west. Party critics called him an opportunist; he retorted that it was they who were the opportunists, desiring to score swift victories, at the cost of large numbers of soldiers, which would all too quickly turn into futile defeats.

In the arguments and meetings that followed, Mao found new support from his sometime nemesis Zhou Enlai, who knew from personal experience that while Mao could often be abrasive, he was usually right on strategy. He still found Mao unreliable, but he began to treat his military acumen with more respect. But Mao was reprimanded by higher-ups, and decided to have another 'illness'.

For those like Mao in the Chinese Soviet Republic area who chose to ignore unfavourable orders, their very successes could lead to new problems. Mao and his colleagues had been so successful in establishing a base at Ruijin that it became the new Communist headquarters, putting all the troublesome Party officials within walking distance. Upon their arrival, they began to purge unwelcome elements. It is likely that Mao was only spared because of his honorary position as Chairman of the Republic, and his continuing 'illness' that kept him out of the fray.

Without a role in the army, Mao limited himself to civilian matters, organising a post office and a local currency, and keeping supplies flowing from outside. As ever, his tactics often took the form of banditry with a red flag. Many necessities had to be bought on the black market from Nationalist areas, while some funding came from the 'sale' of revolutionary war bonds: buyers were forced to hand over money in exchange for the worthless pieces of paper.

Mao also drew up laws influenced by the harsh conditions of a military enclave which would endure for decades in the People's Republic. There, for example, was a death penalty for vaguely worded offences such as 'conversation undermining faith in the revolution' and 'counter-revolutionary acts'. There was also the introduction of new voting systems, supposedly designed to render all equal, although in reality, some were more equal than others. All *citizens*, including women, were able to vote from the age of sixteen, an impressively egalitarian decision on paper. However, only the right sorts of people (workers, peasants, soldiers) were designated as 'citizens'; those with a merchant background, the families of former landlords, or families of priests were not permitted to participate.

Mao's other campaign was against marriage itself, and the first law on the statute books of the Chinese Soviet Republic overturned centuries of tradition. It was now officially impossible for young people to be traded like chattels by their parents, as Mao felt he had been in his first marriage. Men and women each had the equal right to make or dissolve a marriage contract; parents no longer had any official say in who married whom. Consequently, the divorce rate among his people skyrocketed, with temporary 'marriages' made and broken with impunity. But for Mao, a divorce was a victory – a sign of a revolutionary struggle against the inequities of patriarchal society. He bragged: 'This democratic marriage system has burst the feudal shackles that have bound human beings, especially women, for thousands of years, and established a new pattern consistent with human nature.'[6] It also led to sexually liberated revolutionary ladies, a phenomenon of which Mao took full advantage, although sex for lower ranks in the army was forbidden.

On previous occasions, Mao had been kept out of military action for only so long as it took one of his replacements to fail spectacularly. But Zhou Enlai and Zhu De, now in charge of the army, kept broadly to Mao's suggested tactics, and in doing so they were able to beat away a fourth encirclement campaign by Nationalist soldiers. This also entailed ignoring several headquarters directives, a fact which did not go unnoticed by Mao. In 1933, he tried to get himself reinstated in a military command, only to be told that recent victories had only been achieved via his exclusion.

Mao could still win political points elsewhere. In September 1933, he and Zhu De entered negotiations with a Nationalist army in the south-eastern province of Fujian.

Mao (third from left) and He Zizhen (far right) with revolutionaries in Jiangxi, around 1933.

As Mao had predicted long before, the presence of the Japanese in Manchuria could be turned to the Communists' advantage. Angry that Chiang Kai-shek had done nothing about the Japanese, some Nationalists were prepared to side with the Communists, and proclaimed themselves a People's Revolutionary Government.

It could have been a major propaganda coup for the Communists, and did distract Chiang Kai-shek from yet another of his campaigns against the rebels, but not even Mao fully believed that the Fujian mutineers were true allies, and when vengeful Nationalist forces descended upon Fujian in November, the Communists offered little support to their alleged comrades.

By 1934, Mao was back on the Politburo of the

Communist Party, although still outnumbered by the rivals that he had termed 'Returning Students' for their habit of pulling of rank on the basis of fancy foreign studies. But all this was less important than the increased threat from Chiang Kai-shek, who had begun a far more effective encirclement campaign, his fifth.

Whereas previously the Nationalists had been dragged down to the Communists' level in the region, forced to march, camp, and make improvised stands, the new policy was to build sturdy stone forts all around Mao's base, from which the Nationalists could mount assaults and, more importantly, arrange retreats. Against a foe without artillery, the 'turtle shell' blockhouses were highly effective, a 'great wall' curving around the north-west of Mao's redoubt for 200 miles. Nor were the bunkers a static line. Nationalist troops would advance forward of each position to build a new blockhouse, gradually inching the line closer to the Communists, until there were more than 14,000 bunkers scattered across the region.

The Communists were slowly hemmed in. Mao repeatedly suggested that the ideal course of action was to run for a new area, thereby rendering the Nationalists' blockhouse construction of the last few months futile. The leadership, however, preferred a futile policy of picking off the Nationalists as they moved from bunker to bunker. According to the Comintern's military adviser, Otto Braun, part of the Communists' problem was that many of their officers had been trained by defectors *from* the Nationalist army, most of whom had learned their own military knowledge from

German manuals that expected an army to advance with high-level support such as airpower and artillery. Such an attitude was entirely unhelpful when working with limited manpower and resources on a guerrilla campaign – something that Mao had been arguing for months.[7]

The piecemeal strategy failed to contain the Nationalist advance, and the Communists showed signs of panic. Execution squads went into battle with regular soldiers, threatening to kill anyone who tried to desert. Meanwhile, many of the civilians in Mao's encampment saw which way the wind was blowing and escaped into Nationalist enclaves, deserting the nascent Chinese Soviet Republic as its borders diminished.

April 1934 saw the Nationalists deliver a crushing defeat to the Communists at Guangchang, north of Ruijin. It was the beginning of the end for the local Communists, since it was now only a matter of time before supply lines to the outside were cut off and the Communists were slowly starved out.

On 15 October 1934, the Red Army did what Mao had been urging all along, abandoning its enclave and running west and north. Hindsight would mythologise this as the 'Long March' that led to victory, but at the time it was a disastrous withdrawal, which propaganda attempted to spin as a decision to head north to fight the Japanese. At the commencement of the march, the Red Army had 86,000 soldiers, 15,000 administrative personnel (including Mao) and a tiny 'nurses' contingent' of twenty-five women, mainly the wives of the leading officials. These included the pregnant He Zizhen. Others were left behind or abandoned *en route*, including Xiao Mao, Mao's two-year-old son by He Zizhen, who was deposited with a wet-nurse and never seen again.[8]

The toughest time for the retreat was the winter of 1934–5, as the starving group walked on, under constant attack from Nationalist forces, including aerial strafing and bombing. If the army had any luck at all, it was that they encountered no resistance from local warlords, who preferred to conserve their own forces in case of an altercation with the Nationalists. Less than half the original number reached the first destination of Zunyi in January 1935.

Mao's struggles within the Party re-emerged at Zunyi. He was the Chairman of a 'state' that no longer existed, and sought a new role in the organisation. 'It was obvious,' wrote Otto Braun, 'that he wanted revenge for the criticism he had suffered':

> Now there emerged the possibility – years of partisan struggle had been directed at bringing it about – that by demagogic exploitation of isolated organisational and tactical mistakes, but especially through concocted claims and slanderous imputations, he could discredit the Party leadership and isolate [the] General Secretary.[9]

Mao managed to get himself appointed to the Standing Committee of the Politburo, but also worked on Zhou Enlai, the Party official with whom he enjoyed such a fractious, hot-and-cold relationship. Zhou named him as his military adviser. Mao was back in the army, albeit peripherally.

Further setbacks dogged the army through February, including unwelcome battles with warlords and Nationalists. He Zizhen gave birth to a girl during the retreat, and was forced to leave her with a peasant family. The baby was not even named, and died soon afterwards. However, the hardships of the withdrawal, and the immense loss of life, also served to thin down Mao's opposition. By spring 1935, the Red Army now resembled the Zhu–Mao army of old, with Zhu De as military leader, and Mao as its political officer. Mao's reinstatement as a strategic planner meant the unfortunate policy of engaging the foe directly was soon discarded. Instead, the Red Army returned to his preferred guerrilla tactics, with Mao's role growing not only in fact, but also in reputation, thanks to the distribution among other groups of his writings on warfare.

The Nationalists tried to fight back with writings of their own, including propaganda announcing that Zhu De was dead, and that Mao's legendary 'illness' was a genuine affliction that threatened to kill him. Nor was the Long March an idea accepted without complaint by the soldiers. Mao faced another of the periodic criticism sessions, during which a group of the Party elite suggested that his strategy of walking out of danger was taxing the men's health.

By the time the Red Army reached relative safety, their numbers had fallen to barely 20,000. Disease, exhaustion, and desertion had whittled away the troops, but those who remained were proven to be tough, resilient, and committed. There was, however, still little sense of a final destination; the Red Army was reacting to the pursuit of the Nationalists, not aiming for a decisive victory elsewhere. By May 1935, the marchers were on the very edge of China, marching north past Huili, and climbing ever higher until they reached the uneven plateau country of the Yi people.

Like many other ethnic peoples in China's periphery, the Yi were no friends of the Han who formed the Chinese majority. This could be turned to the army's advantage against the Nationalists, but did not ensure that the Communists an easy time of it either. The peasant soldiers of the Red Army found themselves dealing with primitive, tribal locals. One Party grandee secured their safe passage by participating in a ceremony where he drank chicken's blood with a local tribal leader, but Yi scavengers still murdered some of the Communists' less able soldiers.

Once through Yi territory, the Red Army faced its greatest risk, crossing the Dadu River. Although a few small boats were available, Mao realised that most of the soldiers would have to cross further upstream, where a precarious chain-link bridge spanned a hazardous gorge. According to legend, the army's forward group was forced to clamber along the 120-yard bridge in the face of Nationalist machine guns. A handful of soldiers successfully ran the gauntlet and got within grenade-throwing range of their enemies. These soldiers then made a miraculously lucky escape. But the story of this 'battle' at the bridge over the Dadu is highly questionable. Most modern Chinese base their knowledge of it on the heroic re-enactment made for television propaganda; most non-Chinese on the highly apocryphal account which Mao gave to Edgar Snow. Some surviving witnesses now claim that the battle never took place, that Nationalist defenders were nowhere near, and that none of the 'suicide squad' that took the bridge was even wounded. But if the battle at the bridge never took place, it calls into question much of the other received wisdom about the Long March. Mao, ever the classical scholar, couched it as a *Journey to the West* like his favourite childhood book: a long, picaresque quest in search of betterment. Others have suggested that the Long March was not merely a retreat, but a retreat that played right into the hands of Chiang Kai-shek, who even steered it to his own ends.[10]

By 'pursuing' them but never quite wiping them out, Chiang was able to send his army deep into Sichuan and Yunnan, regions whose loyalty to the Nationalists was questionable. Communist history paints the Long March as a victory, yet it remains possible that at least some of the Communists' lucky escapes were engineered by the Nationalists as an underhand means of sending troops to pacify hostile areas without having to seek permission from local warlords.

Finally, on 12 June 1935, forward units of the First Army ran into a group of unknown soldiers in Dawei, a small village outside Maogong, Sichuan. They immediately began shooting, only to recognise their enemies' bugle calls as Communist signals. The First and Fourth armies had finally met up. The death toll, however, was severe. Only 15,000 of

The bridge over the Dadu River at Luding.

Mao's original 86,000 survived, many of them wounded. He Zizhen, for example, had been severely injured during a strafing by Nationalist planes, and was barely clinging to life.

Of more political concern was the matter of what to do next. Mao's army, exhausted and badly battered, now found itself alongside Communist allies in a notably better state of health. The Fourth Army's leader, Zhang Guotao, was of equivalent rank to Mao, and there had been no communication from their superiors for months. Even if the Party had been able to establish contact with Communist agents back in the distant cities, a Nationalist raid had seized the

Mao photographed with Zhu De at Yan'an, 1937.

Party's radio transmitter, once again forcing much longer communication lines through old-fashioned messengers. It was no longer clear who was in charge, and Mao and his rival leader had to work things out between themselves.

Before long, it became clear that Zhang and Mao had radically different ideas about the next step. Arguments and meetings stretched over several weeks, as Party committees attempted to reach a mutually acceptable plan. Eventually it was decided that each army continue on its separate way until orders to the contrary arrived from their superiors.

After a gruelling march across swampy grasslands, in which many more soldiers died of dysentery and typhus, the two armies fell out once more, with Zhang ordering a retreat. Amid heated arguments among officers and advisers, Mao's First Army set out alone. Eventually, it was a Nationalist newspaper that inadvertently supplied them with a destination. Plans had been afoot to keep walking until they reached Russia itself, but First Army members read about a Communist enclave in north-west China.

Just over a year after the Long March began, the 5,000 survivors of Mao's epic journey limped into their new home on 22 October 1935, the paltry numbers marginally swelled by new recruits that had not experienced the full march. They found themselves in the arid desert landscape of Bao'an and, later, Yan'an, where local people dwelled in caves cut into sandy cliffs. It was a forbidding, unpleasant place, but it was relatively safe from the Nationalists, and would be Mao's base for more than a decade.

The World at War

Mao had not been long in Yan'an before he was searching for new ways to continue the conflict. He saw Japan's belligerence, which had coerced Chiang Kai-shek's government into such intensely embarrassing concessions as a 'goodwill mandate' that made it a crime to criticise Japanese activities, as an opportunity. North-east China was falling steadily under Japanese influence, and Mao wanted to exploit the hatred non-Communists felt towards the invaders.

In November 1935, Mao began writing to Zhang Xueliang, the warlord who controlled much of Manchuria. Zhang Xueliang's father was the 'Old Marshal' Zhang Zuolin, a warlord who had ruled north-west China and nominally supported the Nationalists, but also permitted many concessions to the Japanese. Beaten out of Manchuria after the Old Marshal's murder, Zhang's surviving forces initially fought the Communists in north China, before his change of heart; a defection largely inspired by his desire to have the Communists aid him where the Nationalists had not, in driving the Japanese from his homeland. Although nominally an ally of the Nationalists, Zhang responded swiftly to offers of a pact with the Communists in order to allow both sides to concentrate on defeating the greater enemy, Japan. Zhang refused to openly defy Chiang Kai-shek, but he agreed in principle with many of Mao's aims.

Mao at his writing desk at Yan'an after the Long March.

The two leaders struck a deal to avoid attacking each other, and Zhang even ensured that his Communist 'enemies' were supplied with new weapons.

With barely a couple of months to recover from the Long March, the survivors of Mao's First Army were on the move again for the 'Eastern Expedition to Resist Japan and Save the Nation'. Its title was brilliant propaganda, highlighting Communist willingness to engage the Japanese while the Nationalists allegedly cowered in fear. However, the reality was less impressive – none of the First Army's military actions between February and May 1936 were directed at the Japanese. Instead, it crossed the Yellow River into Shanxi province to fight a series of skirmishes with Nationalists, while hoping to recruit new soldiers and acquire money by the usual extortionate means.

Despite continued hostilities between their forces, and

general Party agreement that Chiang Kai-shek would ultimately need to be removed, Mao recommenced making overtures to the Nationalists. In particular, he sent messages to an anti-Japanese faction within the Nationalist party, hoping to uncover support against Chiang. Meanwhile, anti-Japanese demonstrations continued to grow throughout China, often with Communist support. While talks progressed, Mao also began courting some of the industrial powers. It had not escaped his notice, for example, that Japan and the United States were drifting apart, and to someone of Mao's pragmatism, it was worth cultivating potential allies even among the imperialists. This new campaign did not use traditional negotiators. Instead, the Communists permitted the journalist Edgar Snow to visit their encampment at Yan'an. The resultant book, *Red Star Over China*, made the Chinese Communists famous all over the world. Its title in Chinese translation, much to Mao's likely glee, would be *Stories of a Journey to the West*, echoing that of his favourite childhood story.

A journalism-school dropout from Missouri, Edgar Snow had arrived in China in 1928. He found a job with the *China Weekly Review* in Shanghai and became a teacher at Yenching University in Beijing. He toured China on projects for the Nationalists' Ministry of Railways, and became the first foreign journalist to visit the Communists in Yan'an.

Mao took the opportunity to get his message across to the outside world, knowing that it would also reach the Nationalists. He told Snow that 'the revolutionary task is not immediate socialism, but the struggle for independence. We cannot even discuss communism if we are robbed of a country in which to practise it.'[1] But although there were a few attempts at reconciliation, Chiang Kai-shek was in no mood to hear Mao's latest pleas for a pact. He suspected (perhaps rightly) that it was another Communist trick, and (wrongly) that a Nationalist victory against the Communists was within his grasp.

When talks broke down, Mao's would-be ally Zhang Xueliang took matters into his own hands. He ordered a group of his men to kidnap Chiang Kai-shek. Although Nationalist bodyguards fought off the attack, Chiang was later found hiding on a hillside in his nightshirt, and taken into custody by Zhang Xueliang's men. But Zhang neither wanted to execute Chiang, nor give him the show-trial that Mao hoped for. Instead, he merely hoped to convince him to change his policy; heavy-handed 'persuasion', certainly, but that was nothing unusual in China.

The plot stumbled, not helped in the slightest by Moscow's decision to endorse the Nationalists instead of supporting Zhang. Following Moscow's change of heart, Mao sent negotiators in to secure Chiang's release, thereby managing to have associates on both sides of the kidnapping. The kidnapper now became the captive, as Zhang Xueliang was sentenced to ten years in prison. In principle, however, the Communists had won an important assurance: Chiang's promise under duress that he would arrange a truce between them and the Nationalists, in order to unite against the Japanese.

Mao with He Zizhen, Yan'an 1937.

On 7 July 1937, Japanese soldiers seized the Marco Polo Bridge, a crucial railway junction only five miles from Beijing. Although Chiang Kai-shek had tried to turn a blind eye to Japanese infiltrations in Manchuria, an enemy incursion so close to China's capital could not be ignored. Japan and China were at war. By 29 July, Japanese forces were in Beijing itself, and the capital's port, Tianjin. The following month, they attacked Shanghai, forcing Chiang Kai-shek to make good on his promise. The Nationalists announced that the new Nationalist 'Eighth Route Army' would aid resistance against the Japanese. The name was a new designation for the Communists.

Mao's personal life was not so victorious. His wife, He Zizhen, still had chunks of Nationalist shrapnel in her body, and had borne Mao four children, of whom only one, daughter Li Min, had not been abandoned as an infant. Meanwhile, He and other veterans of the Long March faced competition for their men's affections from new arrivals at Yan'an. Her pre-occupation with rearing their daughter was probably the last straw: Mao had affairs elsewhere, and the couple were soon living apart. He Zizhen left him in spring 1937, setting off for Shanghai, but eventually ending up in Moscow in October 1937. There, she received treatment for her remaining wounds from the Long March, and also gave birth to Lyova, her last child by Mao, a boy who soon died of pneumonia. Her understandable depression was magnified when Mao ordered her to remain in Russia to convalesce, and in 1939 she heard the inevitable news that someone else, Jiang Qing, was now living with Mao as his wife. Suffering a breakdown, she was committed to a mental asylum and did not return to China for nearly a decade.

Meanwhile, Mao busied himself with Jiang Qing, a flighty, unpredictable twenty-three-year-old actress who had already had two previous husbands since running away from home to join the theatre seven years earlier. Jiang Qing became Mao's wife on the understanding that

Jiang Qing, right (1914–91).

she would stay out of the limelight: a directive that was to prove unbearable for a performer. She gave birth to Mao's last known child, their daughter Li Na, in August 1940. The couple were estranged by 1942, and Mao was heard to say that he had 'rushed' into what was effectively a marriage of convenience, but Jiang Qing remained his official companion for the rest of his life. In her later years, she descended into hypochondria and political intrigue, while Mao continued to have affairs with other women.

Struggles continued among the Communists with the arrival of Wang Ming in Yan'an. Wang was a Comintern appointee who liked to imply that he spoke with the backing of Moscow. As had happened before, Mao faced a political rival who insisted on direct conflict with the Communists' enemies. Mao, however, continued to cling to his successful guerrilla policy.

Words formed an important part of the internal battle line. While China fought Japan, Mao spent several months in 1938 writing two treatises on guerrilla warfare. Ostensibly designed to aid in the battle against the Japanese, they also reminded the Party of his successes. Mao rightly suspected that even the combined Nationalist and Communist forces would be unable to halt the main Japanese advance. Mao predicted a series of minor Japanese victories, and called for the Chinese to prepare for them, awaiting the moment when the Japanese lines of communication and supply would be overstretched.

One Communist faction pressed for further *détente* with the Nationalists, but Mao continued to regard the latter as unreliable allies who would turn on the Communists as soon they could; the feeling was probably mutual. Mao's writings on guerrilla tactics tacitly prepared his faction not only for a prolonged war against the Japanese, but also for the subsequent showdown with the Nationalists. Back in Moscow, the Comintern agreed, and their support reinforced Mao's Party position.

Publicly, Mao gave the impression that he was burying the hatchet, but he still intrigued against his perceived enemies. Simply by dint of still being alive, and with the added bonus of Russian backing, he could imply that his way was the correct way. He made a veiled attack on the Returned Students, again hinting that their foreign trips and their book-learning could never compete with direct experience – his experience. In doing so, he made a claim that only the Chinese could create a Communism that was

Mao making an anti-Japanese speech to students at Yan'an, 1938.

suitable for China: 'If a Chinese communist, who is part of the great Chinese nation, bound to it by his own flesh and blood, talks of Marxism in isolation from Chinese characteristics, that Marxism is a mere abstraction. Therefore the sinification of Marxism ... making sure that its every manifestation has an indubitably Chinese character, is a problem that the whole Party must understand and solve without delay.'[2] More than ever before, Marxism and Communism in China were whatever Mao said they were.

Mao's prediction of Nationalist perfidy was unsurprisingly correct. Already, by January 1939, Chiang Kai-shek's government had approved a secret decision to make life as difficult as possible for their Communist allies. As Communists and Nationalists waged separate wars against the Japanese, the united front policy faltered at several points during 1939 and 1940. The worst disgrace was conducted against the New Fourth Army, a group of former guerrillas and partisans comprising the forgotten divisions who had stayed in south China to cover the rear while others made the Long March. A week of ambushes and battles left 9,000 of them captured or killed by their supposed allies.

Shortly after the massacre of the New Fourth Army, Mao made political moves of his own, commencing what would be later known as the Yan'an Rectification Campaign in September 1941. Announcing a series of efforts to ensure that the Party was not corrupted by 'bad ideas', he initiated a barrage of purges against rivals within the Communist leadership. Yet again, he argued that experience was more important than theory.

Mao's outdated Confucian education left him permanently resentful and jealous of those with modern knowledge, qualifications, or any experience of languages and cultures beyond China, even though modernisation was increasingly seen as vital, and Russian Marxism was supposedly the guiding light of the Chinese Communists. This strange contradiction was a defining factor in Mao's own philosophy. With its wilful ignorance of foreign matters, and its dogged insistence on a Chinese way that only a Chinese person with experience of the Chinese countryside could comprehend; with its blinkered concentration on many qualities that a person should *not* possess, Maoism was, quite literally, a creed that only Mao could have created.

'We have comrades,' Mao said, 'who have a malady, namely that they take foreign countries as the centre and act like phonographs, mechanically swallowing whole foreign things and transporting them to China.'[3] This was not just about trouncing the Returned Students, who were already defeated. Mao was laying the foundations of his defence for the next challenge, whether it came from within the Party or abroad. In doing so, he was sowing the seeds of many later political decisions and atrocities.

One victim of the Yan'an Rectification Campaign was Wang Shiwei, an intellectual who dared to point out in 1942 that all were not equal at Yan'an: the political officers had better clothes and food, and the supposed liberation of Communist women only liberated the pretty ones so they could climb into bed with the leaders. Wang's comments angered Mao, who decreed that the writer was a parasite upon the revolution, betraying his vocation by not serving the needs of the Party (whatever that meant, which was, of course, whatever Mao as Party leader wanted it to). Wang was put on trial for his unwelcome comments, and accused of being a Nationalist agent sent to undermine the Party. His supporters melted away, and he was eventually imprisoned. He would die five years later, executed by a local warlord who hated intellectuals.

Wang was not the only one. Mao's henchman Kang Sheng was permitted to investigate any real or imagined attacks on the Party in a series of witch-hunts that saw a thousand suspected spies held and questioned. The charade was eventually wound up in December 1943, when Zhou Enlai returned to Yan'an and queried Kang Sheng's zeal. In the bitter aftermath, less than one in ten of the accusations was upheld, although more than half had confessed to non-existent crimes under interrogation and torture.

However, the tensions between Communists and Nationalists were subsumed within an even larger united front as several conflicts around the world grew into the Second World War. Until 1941, the conflict in China had been a local matter, but the Japanese alliance with the Nazis and attack on Pearl Harbor put China on the side of the Americans, British, and other Allied powers. As Mao had predicted earlier, the Communists found new and unlikely friends in the form of the self-same imperialists against whom they had once demonstrated.

With the Russians entering the war against the Nazis, Stalin had to maintain a united front with the Western powers, and disassociate himself from accusations of intrigue abroad. Soviet Russia therefore abandoned its 'Communist International' (Comintern) scheme, which meant that Mao's lifelong insistence on Chinese principles for the Chinese Party gained new lustre. Elsewhere, Chiang Kai-shek published a book, *China's Destiny*, in which he implied that he was already the leader of China. It became a textbook all over Nationalist China; the Communists fought back by using Mao's works as a textbook, too. This encouraged an entire youthful generation to regard him as an infallible statesman, helped sow the seeds of the Cultural Revolution of the 1960s and, once and for all, established Mao as the leader of the Chinese Communists.

Although many of its members seemed to mistake the Communists for yet another new faction, the Party enjoyed growing support and solidity. Mao started to take on the accoutrements of an emperor. His face was depicted surrounded by the rays of the sun, songs were sung in his honour, and he even participated in agrarian rituals, such as planting the first grains of millet in the spring of 1944.

Mao stood to benefit not only from the continued battles of distant Chinese forces against the Japanese, but also from victories further afield, against the Nazis. The Nationalists and Communists might never have defeated the Japanese, but now that Japan was America's enemy, too, they could expect some help. The Nazis began retreating in Europe in 1944, and the expectation that Japan would be next.

If Mao had been counting on Russian friendship, he was in for a surprise. Russia held back from fighting in Asia until it was all but over. An American atom bomb had already obliterated Hiroshima before Russia formally declared war on Japan, hoping to acquire territory without going to the unpleasant trouble of fighting over it. Even as the war stumbled to a close, with every indication that Japan would be banished from Chinese soil, the Communists saw their supposed Russian allies dealing directly with the Nationalists. The Russians and Americans both continued to regard Chiang Kai-shek as the rightful ruler of China, although both paid lip-service to the idea that the Communists should play a role in its democratic future.

With the departure of Japan, China returned to the state it was in back in 1937, with the Nationalists and Communists at each other's throats. Now, however, the Communists were considerably greater in number. The Nationalists had spent large parts of the war hiding out in south-west China, whereas Communist partisans had been in the thick of the fighting. There were many remote Chinese villages that had not seen a Nationalist for five years, but were well aware of the Communists in their neighbourhood.

The time had come to finish the civil war postponed by the Japanese invasion. Mao ordered Lin Biao to attack Nationalist armies in Manchuria in March 1946, and before long uprisings and further conflicts were breaking out all over China. Mao was able to count on secret Russian aid, often in the form of captured Nazi or Japanese weapons, and even gained new troops and educators from among the ranks of Japanese prisoners of war. In March 1947, after over a decade in Yan'an, Mao and the Party leaders left their makeshift capital, ready to take the fight to the Nationalists once and for all.

Chairman Mao

The Chinese civil war, which lasted in isolated areas until 1950, represented a major change in Mao's policies. Formerly, the Communists had fought a guerrilla war, attacking their enemies at the margins, but never intending to hold territory. Also, in the past, Mao had kept the Red Army as a rural force, and much of the countryside was already Communist. Now the time had come to seize the cities, and with them their resources, the communication networks, and the country.

Mao had better support than before, and he had better assets, including artillery. Meanwhile, the Nationalists had grown lazy or despondent. Moreover, at least officially, the Communists were all volunteers fighting against unwilling Nationalist conscripts. That is not to say that there were not inept, cowardly Communists, or skilled, brave Nationalists, but simply that the volunteer image was a propaganda victory of its own. As the Nationalist resolve began to crumble, there were several high-profile defections, which only added to Chiang Kai-shek's paranoia.

With the Japanese out of the way, Mao went back to his old tricks. Peasant collectives were encouraged to turn on their enemies, spelling swift ends for former collaborators, landlords, and anyone else who did not toe the Party line. Such purges were not mere local quarrels, but part of the Communist policy of returning the land to the people, and earning more support from the peasants who farmed it.

In late 1948 and early 1949, the Communist advances were undeniable. Lin Biao led armies on Beijing itself, while Nationalist defections both depleted Chiang's army and added to that of Mao. The World War might have been over, but almost two million Chinese died in the subsequent civil conflict. Most of them were Nationalists. By the end of January 1949, Beijing had fallen, and Chiang Kai-shek was in full retreat. The Communist forces pressed south, across the Yellow and Yangtze rivers, taking Nanjing by April and Shanghai by the end of May. Chiang, however, had an escape plan, and led the remnants of his Nationalist army, navy, and air force off mainland China and to Taiwan. Their descendants remain there to this day, referring to their island bastion as the 'Republic of China'.

The sudden departure of the Nationalists delivered China to the Communists, who now had to make good on their years of planning. But just as Mao's warfare was based not on conquest but attrition, the general policies of the Communist leaders had focused on winning power, not on any consensus about what to do next.

It was not lost on Mao that the Communists had only acquired many of China's cities by default, through the retreat of the Nationalists, not through any local uprising of their own and hence not through any spirited awareness of class consciousness or Communist beliefs. Such cities, Mao felt, would be the most likely to resist the imposition of Communism, since it would indeed have to be

Chiang Kai-shek and his wife Soong Mei-Ling in 1937.

imposed upon them, rather than evolving out of their own revolutionary spirit.

Mao announced a 'people's democratic dictatorship', emphasising that the formerly oppressed were now in charge. All major industry was nationalised, and foreign-owned companies were 'restored' to Chinese ownership. 'Who are "the people"?' he wrote. 'At the present stage in China, they are the working class, the petty bourgeoisie and the national bourgeoisie. Under the leadership of the Communist Party, these classes unite together to ... carry out a dictatorship over the lackeys of imperialism.'[1]

The People's Republic of China (PRC) was officially founded on 1 October 1949, when Mao stood at Tiananmen, the Gate of Heavenly Peace from which the emperors of old had issued their proclamations. His own proclamation announced a new order:

> The Chinese people, comprising one quarter of humanity, have now stood up. The Chinese have always been a great, courageous, and industrious nation; it is only in modern times that they have fallen behind ... [Today] we have closed ranks and defeated both domestic and foreign aggressors ... Ours will no longer be a nation subject to insult and humiliation ... We, the 475 million Chinese people, have stood up, and our future is infinitely bright.[2]

The announcement to a crowd of 100,000 was followed by a military parade, and chants of 'Ten thousand years to Chairman Mao', a wish of oddly imperial flavour. Nationalist resistance continued far to the south-west, but with Chiang Kai-shek gone, the remainder of the civil war was gradually fizzling out.

Despite the Soviet government's earlier refusal to believe that the Chinese Party, with its rural rather than urban focus, represented a properly communist force for change, it was the first foreign power to recognise the PRC. Mao made a brief trip to Moscow in December, but was guarded in his dealings with the Russians, saying to a Soviet politician: 'There are real friends and false friends. False friends are friendly on the surface, but say one thing and mean another ... We shall be on our guard against this.'[3] The Chinese Communists had succeeded in spite of Russian neglect, and Mao would never let his 'allies' forget it.

Mao publicly announced that China would look inward until such time as internal difficulties were sorted out. In fact, there were deeper political issues at stake, since Chiang Kai-shek was still at large. It would, in fact, take almost four decades before most Western powers finally agreed to recognise the Communists as the true rulers of China. The Nationalists on Taiwan would continue to hold the 'Chinese' seat on the UN Security Council until 1971.

Mao was now the titular leader of the most populous force for Communism in the world, albeit a state whose idea of what constituted 'Communism' was already at odds with the beliefs of the Soviet Russians. At fifty-six years of age, he formed a significant element in the small group of men who ruled China, alongside Zhou Enlai and Liu Shaoqi. Although Zhou was now the Premier and Liu the Party's General Secretary, as the Chairman and interpreter of Party doctrine, Mao's power still exceeded theirs.

But despite his august position, Mao still behaved as if he was dealing with a group of surly peasants in a remote village. At least three million people died in the first few years of his regime, while any dissenters were bullied, imprisoned, or forced to recant after brutal 'treatment' for 'sickness' – their only affliction having been to disagree with Mao. Mao's behaviour was despotic and cruel, but he thought it was necessary. China had been in turmoil for almost an entire generation. Production was at an all-time low. The peasant-oriented rhetoric of the revolution acquired new importance when it became clear that the country was on the brink of starvation. It was vital to get the workers back in the fields and the harvest back to pre-Japanese invasion levels, or the Communist utopia would starve to death before it could really begin.

Because Mao would not play along with their version of communism, the Russians left him to it and focused their attempts to advance the cause elsewhere. The Korean peninsula had been a province of Japan for most of the twentieth century. Officials and officers of a native Korean provisional government fought on the side of the Chinese Nationalists during the Japanese invasion of China, and were promised an independent Korea 'in due course' by the Cairo Declaration in 1943. Soviet Russia complicated matters by invading Korea as an Allied power, causing the country to be partitioned upon the Japanese surrender in 1945, with a border along the 38th Parallel. The division led to the establishment of two rival governments, that of the Soviet-backed Kim Il-sung in the North, and the

American-backed Syngman Rhee in the South, both claiming to be the legitimate rulers of the entire peninsula.

Mao was warned that Stalin had approved a move to 'reunify' the Korean peninsula, which had been split between a Russian-backed north and an American-backed south since World War Two. The northern leader, Kim Il-sung, attacked the south on 25 June 1950, obliging Mao to offer, at the very least, limited support as a fellow Communist. Mao was forced to call off his plans to retake Taiwan, and move several divisions north to the Korean border. Kim Il-sung's impressive advances into the south were a little too fast for Mao's liking. Mao and his fellow Chinese leaders had a lifetime of experience fighting overconfident invaders, and warned Kim Il-sung to slow down. Kim carried on regardless, leaving his forces wide open to a surprise attack by American forces led by General Douglas MacArthur. The amphibious landing at Incheon, Seoul's seaport, cut the supply lines of the North Koreans, and in the protracted conflict that followed, the American-backed South Korean forces not only pushed the North Koreans back over their original border, but kept on going.

The issue of Korean 'reunification' was now reversed. Instead of supporting a North-led attempt to conquer the South, Mao was compelled to prevent a South-led attempt at conquering the North. Mao was intensely reluctant to get involved; Korea was not his problem, and he would have preferred to deal with Taiwan and then continue rebuilding China after its two generations of warfare. He also suspected, rightly, that the Russians would never make good on their promises of military aid.

As Russia and the United States established themselves as post-war superpowers, Korea was to become the first 'proxy war', in which the giants duelled using other nations as their champions. Neither superpower wanted to be seen as an open aggressor, since such an admission might lead to direct conflict, and in the wake of Hiroshima, even atomic war. Instead, the US continued to operate under a United Nations mandate in Korea, while Soviet aid was muted. In the meantime, Mao was forced to commit thousands of troops to aid in the defence of North Korea, which he did on the pretext that the Chinese reinforcements were an expeditionary force of volunteers, and not an official Chinese invasion.

Mao similarly intervened in Tibet, a former imperial possession which had previously excluded all ethnic Chinese from its territory after the 1911 revolution. Communist China 'liberated' Tibet by invading in 1949. The Tibetans appealed to the United Nations and the British in India but to no avail, perhaps unsurprisingly, since the British had signed a treaty with the Manchus as early as 1906 that recognised China's right to rule Tibet. Tibet was forced to sign a treaty in 1951 ostensibly acknowledging its autonomy, but in fact acknowledging China's rule. An uprising in 1959 was brutally crushed and the Tibetan ruler, the Dalai Lama, was forced to flee across the Himalayas to India.

Stalin had already given up on the North Koreans. He

The Panchen Lama, Mao, and the Dalai Lama in Beijing in 1954.

unhelpfully suggested that Mao grant them asylum, and then support guerrilla campaigns from within China. Mao clung grimly to the idea of at least hanging onto the 38th Parallel – the original North–South Korean border – and ultimately did so, despite astoundingly limited resources.

The Korean War dragged on for two more years, until the death of Joseph Stalin and the election of Dwight

Eisenhower changed the political situation. By 1953, the border between North and South was much the way it had been before, at the cost of hundreds of thousands of lives – 140,000 of them Chinese. One of the casualties was Mao's eldest son, Anying, whose death was kept from Mao for two months in order to prevent it affecting his political decisions. Anying was killed in a napalm strike on Tongchang County in November 1950, his body burned beyond all recognition and identified only by his Soviet wristwatch, which had been a gift from Stalin. The news of his death was kept secret from the Chairman until January 1951, when it became impossible to maintain the fiction any longer. Rumours about the incident have long alleged that Anying, serving under a pseudonym in the People's Volunteer Army, had flouted the rules by cooking egg-fried rice in the canteen during blackout conditions, and may therefore have made his position an obvious target for enemy bombers. Although the Chinese Academy of History has officially denied the story as mere muck-racking by hostile agents, 'egg-fried rice' remains a sensitive topic on Chinese social media, liable to be censored if posted around the anniversary of Anying's birth or death.[4]

It was an unwelcome lesson for the veterans of the campaign against the Japanese. In the Second World War, China had prevailed by holding their ground against the Japanese. Korea forced Mao and his generals, particularly the long-serving Peng Dehuai, to admit that the nature of war had changed. The USSR and America had vastly greater resources than the Japanese, and were much better equipped to defeat the kind of partisan forces that had survived in China for so long.

Meanwhile, the very fact of Korea had altered the political shape of the Pacific. America now actively supported the Nationalists on Taiwan, and was in the process of turning Japan into an 'unsinkable aircraft carrier'. If Mao attempted to conquer Taiwan now, he would face the kind of fight his forces had barely survived in Korea. The People's Liberation Army (as the Red Army was now called) would have to modernise drastically before it stood a chance against its new imperialist rivals.

War in Korea, like the Japanese invasion, united the Chinese against a common enemy. In 1949, Communist officials had been unwelcome in many parts of China. By 1952, Chinese of both Communist and former Nationalist backgrounds were uniting in their hatred of imperialists. Several foreigners were implicated in alleged spying rings, including one Italian resident who was executed on suspicion of an unlikely plot to assassinate Mao and the Politburo with a mortar attack on the Tiananmen Gate during the anniversary of his proclamation of the People's Republic.[5] Meanwhile, veterans of Korea claimed that the American forces had been testing biological weapons on the battlefield.

Harsh news of the setbacks in Korea served the Communists well at home, allowing further excuses for purges and clampdowns on undesirable elements within the population. Up to two billion US dollars' worth of material was confiscated from private companies in the process of nationalisation – those that remained in private hands were swiftly eroded by 'fines' for non-Communist behaviour. The peasants had been victorious, and now they carried their war into the cities, against their new enemies, the bourgeoisie. 'Oppressors' were to be hunted down and dealt with; a noble enough ideal that, in real life, meant the victimisation of anyone in a position of authority without Communist connections. Unpopular teachers, unloved bosses, and well-to-do businessmen were hauled in front of mass meetings to be criticised and punished, in a series of purges that would lead to thousands more deaths – many, at least officially, by suicide.

The internal conflicts of the 1950s continued the persecutions Mao had unleashed upon the villages in the 1930s, and at Yan'an in the 1940s. Mao's proclaimed dictatorship of the common people was designed to achieve equality, but it did so by dragging everyone down to the same squalid level. Only a few among the Party officials enjoyed the full fruits of Communist power, while at the same time Mao's cronies began to destroy an entire generation of intellectuals and workers who might have saved China.

As the paranoia mounted in Chinese cities, the survivors learned new ways of staying out of trouble. Modernisation was a good thing, in Mao's eyes, but modernisation should emphatically not mean pro-Americanism: anyone with experience or knowledge of the Western world was immediately suspect. The model citizen of Mao's new Republic made no attempt to stand out and paid conspicuous lip-service to the good of the Party – lack of interest in politics was considered a crime, but 'interest' seems to have been defined as complete agreement with the Party line. Intellectuals, said Mao, needed to be 're-educated': cured of their supercilious contempt for the peasants who formed China's new 'elite', an elite that was often starving, violent, and resentful of anyone who was not as poor as they.

One Hundred Flowers

Neglected during the Nationalist era, the old imperial capital of Beijing was refurbished as the centre of the Chinese Communist Party. Not unexpectedly, the best locations were those previously used by the old imperial family, and Mao now dwelled at Zhongnanhai, an estate within the Forbidden City, in a park of lakes and trees. His family's new residence had once been an imperial library; doubtless a source of great pride to the lifelong bookworm.

Idyllic appearances notwithstanding, Mao's household was in a constant state of wariness. The main concern was that the Nationalists would attempt to assassinate him. Now that Mao was out of the countryside and in a known location, security around him needed to be tighter. A personal physician and three concentric cordons of bodyguards kept constant watch, while Mao's food and drugs were supplied from special, high-quality sources, via a double-blind supply process and a poison-taster. Mao's movements were choreographed as part of elaborate protective schemes, his whereabouts often concealed and his means of travel restricted. An armoured train was preferred to a more vulnerable plane for state travel.

One of Mao's primary achievements over forty years of civil war and Party politics had simply been staying alive. Now, in peacetime, he was overstretched. He led a troubled nation of hundreds of millions of people, shattered by two generations of conflict, and in desperate need of a statesman. But the victorious Communist party regularly turned on anyone with genuine abilities. Mao's undeniable knowledge of guerrilla warfare, ancient history, and Party manoeuvring was no help as he was now obliged to reform China from the ground up. He insisted on doing so personally, rounding savagely on any member of the Central Committee who issued orders without first passing them across his desk for approval.

The easy temptation, argued Party officials, was to cling to capitalism, even though it was widely believed in China that faith in capitalism was what had left China beholden to the imperialist powers in the first place. Instead, the Party must now build the Communist utopia everyone had been waiting for, creating a self-sufficient China that did not need to lean on foreign support.

Since 1928, Soviet Russia had embarked on a series of Five-Year Plans, setting itself enormously ambitious targets by which to increase productivity and resource production. The programme inspired Mao and his associates to propose a series of Five-Year Plans of their own, whose goals were designed to push China towards self-sufficiency. Mao estimated, without much evidence, that it would take fifteen years to transform China into a socialist economy, the early phase of which would require farmland to be collectivised – turned from local, individual land-holdings into massive, state-owned areas. Grain production targets, however, were not intended for the immediate benefit of the Chinese people. Mao planned to use grain to barter assistance from the Russians. Since China was still largely a peasant economy, Mao wanted to use the peasants' only output, food itself, to buy the industrial machinery and materials to create the factory areas that would drive the next stage. He would drag China into the twentieth century, even if exporting food would starve millions of his own people.

Private business was expected to work in partnership with the State to achieve Socialism. In return, businesses were 'allowed' to keep 25 per cent of their profits – a polite spin on what was effectively a 75 per cent tax on achievement, alongside continuous suspicion from one's hostile neighbours, who had been inculcated with the belief that private enterprise was wrong.

At the most local level, the Chinese government began a series of initiatives to collectivise farming, parcelling out land equally among the peasantry, and then imposing a system whereby they were made to share the more expensive equipment and materials.

Early years were dogged by a struggle both within the Party and on the collectivised farms over the use of such resources. When things went badly, organisers were blamed for the misuse of manpower and machinery; when things went well, successful peasants would behave as Mao's own father once had, hiring extra workers and buying extra tools, only to incur the wrath of the Party for their capitalist leanings. But human nature persisted. Some landlords slaughtered their own cattle for food rather than see them handed over to other peasants as part of equalisation measures. Nor did many appreciate the removal of surplus grain, not for sale, but for redistribution to other farms which, it was widely believed, were not pulling their weight.

Despite such setbacks, the programme enjoyed more success than it might have, courtesy of a series of better-than-average harvests. Mao originally expected farm collectivisation to take fifteen years. Instead, with a little help from further seizures and persecutions, it was largely implemented by 1956 – at least on paper. Whether the farms would deliver enough food to meet demand was a problem for the future. Convinced that the problems of supplying China were all but over, Mao became overconfident. He reneged on his earlier promise of a mixed economy, in which some private elements were maintained, and approved further attacks on the city bourgeoisie, who were regarded by true Marxists as unreformed relics of imperialism. 'On this matter we are quite heartless!' he wrote. 'On this matter, Marxism is indeed cruel and has little mercy, for it is determined to exterminate imperialism, feudalism, capitalism and small production to boot ... Some of our comrades are too kind, they are not tough enough, in other words, they are not so Marxist ... Our aim is to exterminate capitalism, obliterate it from the face of the earth and make it a thing of the past.'[1]

Railways came next, to move the harvest to where it was needed. Education was brought to the farms to help them utilise their resources better, and health programmes to keep the workers working longer. By 1952, the Chinese government was prepared to claim that China had recovered to the levels of agrarian production it enjoyed before the civil war. Unlike politicians in capitalist democracies, Mao did not really need to concern himself with the need to be re-elected, at least not in the terms that preoccupied Europeans and Americans. For him to hold on to power, he needed to intimidate and cajole the other officials around him, not the public. While other Party officials came and went, he was able to focus on the long-term. Businesses were given until 1957 to nationalise, and Mao could focus on the 'Five-Year Plans' that would keep China steamrollering into the future.

His timing was unfortunate, since, with Stalin now dead, certain Soviets were starting to question the wisdom of some of their own earlier policies. On 25 February 1956 the new Russian leader Nikita Khrushchev dared to suggest that Stalin was not the Communist demigod Party propaganda had made out. Instead, he said that Stalin was a paranoid, brutal dictator who hid behind a personality cult and was responsible for the deaths of untold millions of innocent Russians. Thereafter, Chinese and Russian Communism began to diverge with greater speed. While Khrushchev's criticism might have been justified, it also acknowledged that the Russians were not infallible, and encouraged Mao and his fellow politicians to ignore any Soviet directives with which they disagreed.

Dissatisfaction with the Stalin era did not just cause waves in Russia. Some of Russia's satellite states in Eastern Europe were drifting away from communism, leading to military crackdowns such as the Russian intervention in Hungary in 1956. To Mao, it seemed as if both the Hungarian reformists and the Russian invaders were betraying Communism. Mao continued to insist that the revolution needed to be voluntary for it to succeed. Meanwhile, all over China, those who refused to volunteer were being persecuted.

By 1956, anyone who cared for their survival in Mao's China had learned to keep quiet about anything they did not like about it. The peasant revolution's resentment of anyone who was not a peasant had successfully stifled many potential scientists or engineers, who were unwilling to risk being labelled pro-imperialist as a result of studying foreign knowledge. It also led to silence among Mao's critics, leaving him unsure of whom he should beware.

It was in this environment that Mao suddenly seemed to change his tune. 'Discipline that stifles creativity and initiative should be abolished,' he wrote. 'We need a little liberalism to facilitate getting things done. To be strict all the time won't work.' Mao relaxed his opposition to debate, famously declaring, 'Let a hundred flowers bloom, let a hundred schools of thought contend.'[2]

Those who had lived through so many years of purges were, naturally, suspicious. One visible sign of change was that a few bold women dared to wear something other than the homogenous peasant uniforms promoted by the Party, but Mao demanded that China must be as hard on itself as he was on himself in private, eternally criticising, seeking to improve, in a state of constant revolution. Just as the PRC's Marriage Law regarded divorce as a victory against spousal evil, so Mao claimed to want more criticism. The Russians had already demonstrated that not everything done in the name of Communism was perfect, and Mao warned against complacency within the party itself. In hindsight, his terms were chillingly reminiscent of the Yan'an Rectification Campaign. 'There are times when nothing but a beating can solve the problem,' he wrote. 'The Communist Party has to learn its lesson ... We must be vigilant, and must not allow a bureaucratic work style to develop. We must not form an aristocracy divorced from the people.'[3]

Immediately, there were complaints against Mao, particularly from intellectuals who did not appreciate his policy on the arts. Although Mao was bound to express his disdain for the comments themselves, he would surely register his broad approval for the circulation of ideas – after all, he said, 'Truth stands in contrast to falsehood and is developed out of the struggle against it. Beauty stands in contrast to ugliness and is developed out of the struggle against it ... In short, fragrant flowers stand in contrast to poisonous weeds, and are developed out of the struggle against them.'[4]

Mao said that ignorance left people open to suggestion. He would prefer it, he claimed, if the works of Chiang Kai-shek were available in Communist China, so that the people were able to know their enemy. He later changed his mind about this, and ordered Chiang's books to be only available in censored editions.

Many mistrusted Mao's honeyed words. It was hard to believe that the man who had once ruined Wang Shiwei's career in Yan'an over accusations that the bigwigs had better food and more fashionable clothes would suddenly permit 'healthy debate'. Some wary Chinese suspected that the 'Hundred Flowers' policy would only be allowed to flourish for as long as it served Mao's purposes, and that anyone pushing too far would mark themselves for a later purge. They were right to worry. Mao gave a four-hour speech on the need for openness, the content of which was unofficially distributed all over China, but at the same time he joked with his inner circle that he was setting a trap: 'How can we catch the snakes if we don't let them out of their lairs?' he said. 'We wanted those sons-of-turtles [bastards] to wriggle and sing and fart ... that way we can catch them.'[5]

He had expected the campaign to reveal a few class enemies worth destroying, but he had also rather hoped that the intellectuals, like the Nationalist soldiers he had set free in his military days, would briefly contend with his philosophy, and then pronounce him a friend.

When the population outside the cities seemed understandably reluctant to voice any criticisms of the Party, Mao even spent three weeks travelling by train through eastern China, persuading local leaders not to be afraid of a little constructive criticism, and to encourage it in their underlings. He even called the editor of the *People's Daily* into his chambers and shouted at him for not getting the Party's message across to the masses. Younger citizens were informed that they would not even be allowed to join the Party unless they could come up with something constructive to criticise about it. All the while, Mao nurtured his killer clause, a rider to the original campaign that noted only criticism that 'strengthened Party leadership' would be acceptable. Anything that promoted 'disorganisation and confusion' (a suitably vague phrase) would not be welcome.

Before long, the criticisms began to arrive, in letters and local newspaper editorials and articles. Unsurprisingly, many of these closely resembled the ones that had brought about the Yan'an Rectification Campaign. Bitter Chinese complained that the revolution had merely propelled a new elite class into power, and that these former barefoot peasants were now well-dressed, well-fed politicians, living lives of luxury while parts of China continued to starve. Some intellectuals pointed out, with equal veracity, the Party's contradictory attitude towards them, cosying up every time it needed their expertise, only to repudiate them for displaying such knowledge. Some even suggested that life for an intellectual had been better under the Japanese occupation – at least then a useful skill had been rewarded with money and status, and not demands from a resentful class of new overlords.

Although occasional apologists would claim that the Hundred Flowers Campaign was an unfortunate experiment that backfired, Mao had planned it all along, at least in some form. What did seem to surprise him was the extent of the criticism that would eventually be unleashed. A few weeks into the campaign, Mao's speeches began to take on a new tone, suggesting that some criticisms were not based on Party loyalties, but a misplaced nostalgia for the days of the old order: in other words, they were anti-peasant, anti-Communist, and, ultimately, anti-Party. At the same time, the call for criticisms reached fever pitch, and complaints appeared that compared the Communists to the Nazis and called for the abolition of the Party itself.

The trap was sprung on 8 June 1957 with an editorial in the *People's Daily*. Whereas the newspaper had once called for comments, now it accused certain sectors of the population of anti-Party behaviour. Mao's four-hour speech was finally published, but in a heavily rewritten form, with a new section that detailed how to tell the 'flowers' from the 'weeds'. It would be used by Party officials against anyone they perceived as an enemy of the Party. 'Weeds' meant not the small numbers Mao had originally expected, but more than half a million people.

In most cases, the sentence was not death. Instead, alleged transgressors were packed off to learn from their mistakes, via re-education programmes that often found them exiled to remote peasant communities for labour reform. Not all victims were even involved with the Hundred Flowers Campaign – in some areas Party officials were simply instructed to root out an acceptable number of suspects in accordance with the national average of 'Rightists', which was determined to be one person out of every twenty.

The effects were devastating. Promising careers were permanently ruined by a combination of penal servitude, deprivation, 'accidents' during 're-education', and suicide, and the damage was compounded when many victims were divorced by their fearful spouses. Even those let off lightly had to deal with the stigma for the rest of their lives; many victims of later purges may simply have been earmarked because of their suspected guilt in this one.

The Great Leap Forward

As the tenth anniversary of the founding of the People's Republic approached, Mao oversaw a series of celebratory architectural wonders in Beijing. These were the 'Ten Great Buildings', including a museum to the ethnic minorities, the Workers' Stadium, and Beijing Railway Station. Two of them, the Great Hall of the People and the National Museum, flanked a newly cleared area in front of the Gate of Heavenly Peace, intended by Mao as a rival to Moscow's Red Square. The new public area derived its name from the gate into the Forbidden City that stood on its north side: Tiananmen Square.

Despite such architectural wonders, the initial impetus of the revolution seemed to be flagging. The workers' cooperatives that had been intended to revitalise the economy were under-performing through corruption, over-confidence, and straightforward bad luck with the weather. The news was disheartening, since agrarian China needed the profits from bumper harvests to fund increases in industrial production. Meanwhile, with Soviet Russia troubled by unrest in Eastern Europe, there was less Russian aid reaching the Chinese.

In 1957, the USSR successfully launched Sputnik 1, the first artificial satellite. The exuberant Nikita Khrushchev made a series of rash promises about forthcoming Soviet achievements that would also shame the capitalist West.

He announced that within fifteen years, Russia's production of iron, steel, coal, electricity, and oil would outstrip that of the United States. Moreover, these incredible (and, as it turned out impossible) industrial leaps would support a vast economy of consumer goods.

Sputnik reminded Mao that there was a world of science and technology beyond his grasp. Western-style chemistry, biology, physics, and their applications were hated imperialist disciplines but now, as the success of their Soviet sometime allies was thrust in their faces, the Chinese suddenly coveted them.

Khrushchev's grand boasts inspired Mao to respond bullishly with some plans of his own. 'We are prepared to sacrifice 300 million Chinese for the victory of the world revolution,' he chillingly announced, writing off half the population of his country in a single statement.[1]

The result was a series of economic disasters that would cause millions of deaths. His first scheme, announced in the same month as Khrushchev's boasts, worked on the principle that much of China's food supply problem was due to unnecessary waste. Mao proposed eliminating the 'Four Pests' – rats, sparrows, flies, and mosquitoes – in a concerted national effort.

The Chinese people complied, most famously with a campaign to kill off every sparrow in China, both by direct hunting and by constantly scaring them away from their natural perches until they eventually dropped from the sky with exhaustion. There were no sparrows the following year to steal grains of wheat, but there were also no sparrows to prey upon the population of caterpillars, resulting in a plague of the insects on China's grain crop.

It would, however, be months before these consequences became apparent, and Mao was already planning other projects. Inspired by Khrushchev's vainglorious schemes, he approved a vast digging scheme for irrigation ditches. Ten million peasants hacked and shovelled a series of canals and reservoirs, their hard work bringing water to previously dry land covering 20 million acres. Their reward for this back-breaking labour was Mao's expectation of increased yields – and now there was even more land for them to work.

At least the irrigation scheme had palpable and predictable results: canals were dug, and water was brought to the crops. Many of Mao's projects in other areas of the economy were more like the ill-fated sparrow-scaring. He announced a Great Leap Forward, confident that China's productive capabilities would surpass Great Britain's within fifteen years. The rashest of Mao's promises concerned an increase in steel output to 40 million tons within that period, and this after the Central Committee had already raised doubts about producing half that amount. Mao chose fifteen years not merely because it represented three Five-Year Plans. It was his best guess of how long he had to live. 'Confucius died at 73', he once observed and Mao hoped to cling on to life just a little longer than the ancient sage.[2]

Mao did not just want to his subjects to benefit from the Communist utopia he had promised them – he wanted to see it himself before he died. In order to do so, he would demand superhuman, often fatal, efforts from the Chinese people. Although Mao was protected by his bodyguards, he was also largely isolated. Security measures ensured that he never got to see everyday people, and his continued estrangement from Jiang Qing kept his surviving family at arm's length. Ultimately, his only encounters outside official business were with his bodyguards and doctors, and with a series of young girls to whom he was introduced at regular Saturday-night 'dances'.

Mao continued to behave like an independent guerrilla rather than the leader of a populous nation. At times, accounts of his actions can make him seen like a confused innocent. In some memos he seems fully aware of China's impoverished state. In others, he seems happy to believe the lies told to him by his underlings. Sometimes he appeared to understand that he was asking the impossible, but on many occasions he seems to have genuinely believed such a leap was feasible, particularly after he returned from a 'fact-finding' mission across China in order to investigate possible approaches, during which he was kept from hearing bad news by a conspiracy of fearful underlings.

In a sense, Mao was a victim of his own success. The Communist scrapper had become a political leader, untutored but supreme. He was doubly cocooned: physically by his paranoia, and mentally by his Confucian education. With his worldview so circumscribed, it is perhaps unsurprising that Mao had a mystical, peasant's view of technology. He treated it not as a discipline of objective facts and testable theories, but as some form of rhetorical device to motivate the people: a magic wand.

For decades, Mao and his colleagues had ridiculed intellectual application as a betrayal of workers' ideals. He had implied, in a hundred different ways, that modern learning (or as he would put it, 'non-Chinese' learning) was of lesser value than hard work in the fields. It was rhetoric that appealed to the peasants, and Mao the peasant farmer's son knew there was little use for chemistry, applied biology, or materials science on a remote subsistence farm. Mao the world leader desperately needed such knowledge, but he refused to recognise that his culture of spite and philistinism had crushed much of the class that could provide it.

Mao was not only overconfident, but also misinformed. Even modern-day Party documents in support of Mao describe his achievements as wondrous before 1948, generally positive before 1957, and then largely disastrous thereafter. His underlings' desire to show him what he wanted to see is at least partly to blame.[3]

In January 1958, though, Mao believed his project was possible, and issued veiled warnings against those who advised caution. Mao was convinced that China would succeed, and that the Party could lead the way, forcing through the changes that were required.

Within fifteen years, Mao wanted China's output to overtake the capitalist nations. He hoped that a generation without a war to fight, for the first time in half a century, would be able to invest all its efforts in rebuilding China. However, Mao seemed unwilling or unable to grapple with the contradictions. He visualised a futuristic nation with high-speed trains and paved roads, its people well-fed and highly educated. He did not seem to devote any thought to how such things could tally with communist philosophy. How could someone study science if he risked assault for his interest in 'imperialist' knowledge? How could a scientist make progress if peer reviews were conducted on political lines, instead of straightforward examination of the facts? How could a woman wear whatever dress she wanted when anything out of the ordinary would lead to a whispering campaign and potential censure?

In August 1958, Mao pushed further, ordering for the establishment of *renmin gongshe* ('people's communes'). To call them *kibbutzim* after the Israeli model would be to imply too much autonomy – instead, they took the loosely organised peasant collectives that had already been imposed and transformed them into much larger bodies.

Mao expressed a nostalgic wish to return to the happy days of Yan'an, where no money was required, since each citizen was supplied, at least officially, according to his needs. Ignoring the fact that the Yan'an experiment had resulted in criticisms of political hypocrisy, it had also taken place on a military base in the middle of a long-running civil war. The Yan'an economy was kept alive by Russian handouts and 'donations' extorted from the surrounding communities. Mao now wanted to impose similar living conditions on rural communities in peacetime China.

The movement from loose collectives to large communes was yet another disaster. At a local level, at least in theory, it was reasonable to expect a farmer to ask his neighbour if he could borrow a rake. It was less reasonable to expect there to be no friction if all rakes were confiscated and held in a central pool, along with all other private property, to be shared out around a community. Such redistribution of wealth even extended to gifts – if relatives sent money or presents from abroad, they would be confiscated and distributed among the collective according to the needs perceived by officials.

Even family life was communised. Children were to be placed in mass crèches, and old people in homes where their care could be managed by a minimal number of workers. These institutions were, predictably, later found to be hellish prisons packed with malnourished inmates. Eating was to be conducted in communal mess halls, so private cooking implements were confiscated.

The breaking of old community and family ties was bad enough, but the fudging required to appease the Party made things worse. Dispossessed workers were now expected to toil in the fields or on other labour projects with no reward beyond a series of vague promises. Their clothing, food, and even entertainment were supposed to be provided by the collective. With commodities in such short supply, and corruption rife from the top down (Mao obviously took far more than he expected one of his own citizens to 'need'), communes simply lied about meeting their targets. The claims led to a form of inflation, not in monetary value, which was irrelevant, but in expectations.

Mao would call for an unrealistic target. Communes would claim to have met it. He would be pleased and make even greater demands. Those communes that had somehow managed to meet the earlier target now found themselves squeezed even harder. Meanwhile, the communes that had lied about their achievements were now assumed to have, for example, high stocks of grain from their harvest schemes. They would be ordered to send some of their non-existent surplus to other communes, and would be forced to lie about that as well.

Mao was insulated from the harsh realities. Although propaganda photographs showed him and his Party associates at work building a new reservoir near Beijing, Mao's involvement lasted barely long enough for the photo opportunity. Unable to meet Mao's unreal targets for steel production, Zhou Enlai encouraged the establishment of backyard furnaces. Before long, small smelting operations all over the country were 'manufacturing' low-grade metal that was next to useless, often by the simple expedient of melting down pre-existing metal items. To fuel the fires, they often used the wooden beams that held up their houses, and the trunks of the trees that grew in their orchards.

This, too, had its unwelcome side-effects. With ninety million people engaged on the futile faking of rural steel production, there were no longer enough workers to manage the crops. Children and students were dragged out of lessons to help in the field, a salutary image for the anti-intellectuals, but a smokescreen to cover a desperate race to save the harvest. Local officials did not help matters by lying about its success.

Peasants claimed that the new, deeper-ploughing experiments they had been instructed to undertake, and the closer planting of crops, were resulting in miraculously high yields in 1958, as much as fifteen times those of 1957. Mao was led to believe the harvest was, in all, twice as bountiful as the previous year's. This was not true. Although 1958's was genuinely the most successful harvest on record, totalling 200 million tons, this fact was not admitted for two decades because it was only half of what the Party claimed. The peasants, assuming that they were living in a time of plenty, made merry with whatever surplus had not been siphoned off to Soviet Russia. Many parts of the country were already facing starvation, and many PLA army units were mobilised to take food to the worst-hit areas.

While news of the lies had been largely kept from Mao, he was all too aware of the famine. Alluding to the classical knowledge that he so often claimed was bourgeois and unnecessary, he suggested that China needed more officials like Hai Rui, an upstanding Confucian minister who had been fired in the 1500s for daring to criticise the Ming Emperor over his treatment of the peasantry – although Mao seemed unwilling to accept such criticism when it did arise. Emboldened, Defence Minister Peng Dehuai brought up the subject of the crops and failed smelting schemes. He was fired for disloyalty. No other member of the Politburo would ever directly challenge Mao again.

Mao played similar games with the Russians, happily discussing a Chinese atomic-weapons programme with Khrushchev while his subjects were diligently melting down their own cooking utensils to impress him. He appeared to take the same blasé attitude to nuclear holocaust as he had to the possibility of 300 million peasant deaths in the Great Leap, saying that a nuclear war that wiped out Russia and America would leave China dominant. This was a front. The Mao who proclaimed the People's Republic had believed that the future of warfare lay in guerrilla campaigns and attrition, but he could see the world had changed. Khrushchev tried to discuss sharing atomic weapons with the Chinese as part of a Communist cooperative force, but Mao saw this for what it was, a direct attempt to influence Chinese military policy, and berated a Soviet diplomat: 'Just because you have a few atomic bombs, you think you are in a position to control us.'[4]

While Khrushchev attempted to steer Mao with the promise of atomic bombs, the Americans sternly hinted that they were not above using them themselves. Hiroshima and Nagasaki had not merely been the closing shots of the Second World War, but the opening salvo of the Cold War, in which America demonstrated to all its potential enemies what fate might await them.

Khrushchev's promise turned out to be hollow. Russia and China were still officially allies and partners in Communism, but increasingly at odds over its implementation. Khrushchev was also a fair-weather friend. China's occupation of Tibet had caused the ruling Dalai Lama to seek asylum in India, leading to increased tensions. August 1959 saw an exchange of fire along the border between China and India, and the death of an Indian soldier. Amid diplomatic protests, Khrushchev remained neutral, preferring to maintain a peaceful state of affairs with the imperialist West.

Mao was furious, regarding this as a betrayal of Communist aims. Khrushchev had urged him to resolve the Taiwan question by negotiation. He had refused to back him up over India, and now he withdrew his support of China's hoped-for atomic-weapons programme. Mao felt deserted, just as he had when Stalin had suddenly sided with the Nationalists. The two heads of government argued over successive meetings of Communist delegates, but the damage had already been done. Mao was confident that China no longer needed to feign friendship with its potential enemies. Khrushchev, for his part, accused Mao of doggedly clinging to ideas that had no place in the modern world, and of a naïve adherence to the letter of Marxist doctrine, rather than its spirit. Mao accused Khrushchev of toadying to the imperialists, a doomed exercise in his view because imperialism would always be in conflict with Communism.

Khrushchev was not going to endure any more lectures on Communism, nor would he help an ally whose attitude was increasingly hostile. In summer 1960, all Russian advisers were ordered out of China. Some 1,400 experts, technicians, architects, and scientists headed back to Moscow. China was on its own, again.

The Cultural Revolution

Russia could not have chosen a worse time to abandon China. The 1960 harvest was significantly less bountiful than that of the previous year. This was not entirely the fault of muddled central planning. A severe drought ruined a third of China's arable land for the year and even lowered the mighty Yellow River.

The famine and shortages that spanned 1959–61 were the worst disaster in Chinese history, killing more than the Second World War or the Taiping Rebellion. Even in those regions where officials survived to report the figures, the death toll was staggering – twenty-five million out of a total population of 600 million is a conservative estimate of the casualties, and some provinces lost a quarter of their population. Many resorted to banditry to steal enough food to survive; others committed suicide or became cannibals. The period saw a drastic drop in the official birth rate. Ostensibly this was because women were too weak to conceive, but many peasant families were eating one another's children. In four provinces and the 'autonomous region' of Tibet, the military suppressed armed uprisings.

Some twenty-five million city-dwellers were deported to the countryside in order to alleviate the problem of supplying urban centres with food when there was no transport. To Mao's intense embarrassment, China's economic miracle backfired so spectacularly that he was obliged to turn to the imperialist west, importing six million tons of grain from Australia, Canada, and Europe in 1961. Even worse, the 'European' supplies had actually originated in the United States – the ultimate loss of face. China would continue to rely on foreign imports for a decade.

Now in his late sixties, Mao officially took a back seat in government. But he was still Chairman, and unwilling to countenance any criticism of his decisions. The new 'leaders', Liu Shaoqi and Deng Xiaoping, proceeded cautiously, only daring to question existing policies when Mao had implied he would agree. The disastrous communal mess-hall directive was revoked in 1961, and prisoners in labour camps were put to work making aluminium cooking utensils to replace all the iron ones that had been destroyed during the ill-fated smelting campaign. Markets were re-opened, allowing peasants to benefit more directly from their labour. Mao also authorised the dismantling of the quasi-military system that grouped villages together in communes, and instead approved a single-village division of labour and responsibility, hoping that peasants would work harder in the presence of their own friends and relatives. In some places, this was simply a rubber stamp for changes that had already taken place as dissatisfied peasants quit communes to farm on their own. 'The peasant wants freedom,' observed Mao, 'but we want socialism.'[1]

It was not until 1962 that Mao came close to admitting his errors. In doing so, however, he was sure to include everyone else: 'Any mistakes that the Centre [of the Party] has made ought to be my direct responsibility, and I also have an indirect share of the responsibility because I am the Chairman of the Central Committee. I don't want other people to shirk their responsibility.'[2]

It was a remarkably terse accounting for the deaths of millions, but the terrible truth of the countrywide famine would be suppressed for long after Mao's death. There was some realisation that the disgraced Peng Dehuai had been right to criticise the Great Leap Forward, but a full admission would have meant Peng's return and the disgrace of those who had not supported him at the time. Peng remained under virtual house-arrest.

By July 1962, however, there were signs that the crop that year would be an improvement. Instead of admitting it was the weather or the slackening of the communal system, Mao saw this as a vindication of his original policy: 'We've been discussing difficulties for two years now,' he said. 'It's become a crime to look on the bright side.'[3] He returned from several months in Hangzhou to reassert his authority in Beijing, angry not only with the partial dismantling of his catastrophic farming policy, but also with the behaviour of his successors towards foreign powers. When left to their own devices, Liu Shaoqi, Deng Xiaoping, and Zhou Enlai, among others, had done what they could to rebuild bridges with other nations, which was vital considering China's food crisis. Mao, however, regarded it as disloyalty, and warned that China risked losing its way on the path of true socialism and becoming like Yugoslavia, a state which, to Mao's mind, was a socialist failure. Mao's concern was that it was only a short step from a return to private farming to a return to private enterprise and the buying and selling of goods for profit, which would in turn mean capitalism and the return of the haves and have-nots.

Revisionism was Mao's new bugbear, and while he fought it at home, isolated clashes continued along the 'autonomous region' of Tibet's border with India. These escalated in October after India's Prime Minister Nehru alluded to parts of Tibet as 'Indian territory'. Mao responded by mobilising 30,000 Chinese troops, who swatted the Indians away in a campaign that lasted only a few weeks. He called it off in November 1962, confident that the Sino-Indian border was one thing which would not be revised.

But the fate of his revolution still exercised Mao. He made a dire prediction that unless something was done to dam the tide of doubt, counter-revolutionary ideas could destroy Chinese Communism in a generation. Mao was sixty-nine years old, and unsure how much longer he would live. He initiated a Socialist Education Movement, designed to drum into the younger generation (and their wavering local leaders) the idea that capitalism had already failed the Chinese, and must not be revived. Old Party members were encouraged to talk about their early experiences, to ensure that everyone appreciated that while life might be hard under Communism, it had been much worse under the warfare and corruption that plagued China beforehand.

It seemed to Mao that the need for re-education went right to the top of the Party – he was deeply unimpressed with the way his nominated successor Liu Shaoqi had handled things while he had been in Hangzhou. Having fallen into Mao's disfavour, Liu's ultimate demise was only a matter of time. Mao's new heir apparent was Lin Biao, the decorated soldier, under whose control the People's Liberation Army had diligently followed Mao's policy (it was easier, after all, to impose a military model on an army). It was Lin Biao who proposed, and later edited, Mao's *Selected Quotations*, the infamous Little Red Book, whose publication in 1964 would revitalise Mao's personality cult. The project seemed to have been conceived to rustle up a single leader's vision for the nation in deliberate answer to Chiang Kai-shek's book, *China's Destiny* (1947), which made similar proclamations on behalf of the exiled Republic. But the Little Red Book was much further reaching in its impact. In a country without religion, it achieved a quasi-biblical status and would even become the tome on which witnesses in a court of law would swear not to lie: 'I promise to Chairman Mao that I will tell the truth.'[4]

In 1964, Mao also embarked on another major campaign, the true nature of which was suppressed until the 1980s. In an increasingly nuclear world, he initiated a Third Front Campaign, designed to create a robust China that would be able to retreat within itself, into shelters and ammo-dumps, all the better to regroup and fight a new guerrilla war against Soviet or American invaders. His Third Front scheme was a secret, nationwide project that would last for fifteen years, diverting up to half of the nation's annual budget to the construction of fall-out shelters, mountain redoubts, and protected power plants and factories in the remote hinterland.[5] Because knowledge of the general project was so heavily suppressed, it became a matter of myth and rumour. Baffled locals would speak of their unexpected corvée labour obligations digging a new reservoir, or working in an unspecified factory. Beijing, it was said, boasted a tunnel network the length of the Great Wall, much of which has since been repurposed as the basis of some of its metro lines and stations.

Meanwhile, Mao commenced a new assault on his enemies. His target was *Hai Rui Dismissed from Office,* a play written by the Beijing mayor Wu Han, ostensibly to educate the masses about Mao's earlier pronouncement that China needed more Hai Ruis. It was widely regarded not as a work supporting the Communist regime, but as a piece of subtle criticism, with Mao symbolised by the unheeding emperor, and the unfortunate Peng Dehuai signified by the noble official who stood up to him. Mao arranged to have an attack on the play published in November 1965.

It seems such a minor act compared with some of the great sweeping changes that had been imposed in past years. But in confronting *Hai Rui Dismissed from Office*, Mao was launching an attack on Peng Dehuai's known associates, as well as Beijing's mayor and his Party allies. Mao intended to take the purge further, searching out all those counter-revolutionaries who wished to follow Khrushchev's ungrateful Russian lead and turn on their elders. His chosen weapon was a generation of students born at the same time as his beloved People's Republic. Mao encouraged an official within the Beijing University philosophy department to put up a poster criticising the university president, then turned up in person, endorsed the comments, and ordered its contents broadcast on national radio.

Reared on a diet of Mao's thought, waving his Little Red Book and encouraged to turn on counter-revolutionaries, Chinese teenagers carried out Mao's campaign for him. Some did it out of quasi-religious fervour, and others out of idleness, since unemployment in the cities was a growing problem among the young. They were greatly assisted by the free food and rail travel which Mao had just arranged. In effect, Mao unleashed the younger generation on the Party itself. In August 1966, he even gave them an ideological slogan: *Bombard the Headquarters*.

The atrocities of the Cultural Revolution went far beyond the atrocities of the Hundred Flowers Campaign, and where the Great Leap Forward had annihilated the countryside, the Cultural Revolution shattered the cities as well. 'Enemies of the revolution' were rounded up, abused in public, and attacked by the gangs who would soon be known as the Red Guards. The targets included those who were perceived not to be following the socialist aims set out in the Little Red Book, figures of authority regarded as opposing true revolution, and anyone else that the Red Guards didn't like.

In Beijing, the Red Guards' victims were given yin-yang haircuts (half the head shaved), doused in black ink and forced to wear signs proclaiming their crimes. In one school, all but one of the teachers were killed or committed suicide – the lone survivor only escaped because he had once made his pupils laugh in class. In another, the weeping headmistress was doused in scalding water and beaten with improvised clubs. Among a group of persecuted writers and performers, the distinguished author Lao She, sixty-seven years old, suffered a savage beating and drowned himself the following day. The youngest known victim was a six-week-old baby, guilty of having reactionary parents. The Red Guards' victims were variously shot, buried alive, and forced to blow themselves up with explosives.

China's urban youth did not merely kill their elders. They wrecked centuries of priceless cultural artefacts, smashing ancient temples and tearing down 'reactionary' monuments. The grave of Confucius was dynamited, and artworks and paintings destroyed. The mere ownership of an antique was grounds for attack, as was living in one – the monasteries never recovered. In some places, even pet-owners were purged for their feudalist tendencies. Meanwhile, Mao's cronies sent raiding parties in search of known hordes of artefacts and rare books, the thieves disguised as Red Guards.

Lin Biao's selective use of the Little Red Book led to other atrocities. An obscure passage from Mao's juvenilia, written in 1917, was quoted out of context as an argument for burning all books published since the Tang dynasty. Libraries were gutted, and books were burned or pulped to be recycled as Communist-approved works.

Inevitably, the Red Guards turned on each other. The children of peasants regarded themselves as truer revolutionaries than those whose parents were inconveniently well-off. Definitions of acceptability varied wildly. In some places, those with Manchu blood were regarded as evil; in others, local ethnic populations turned on the dominant *Han* Chinese, or vice versa.

It was several months before Mao made much effort to do anything except steer the mayhem. He suggested, for example, in October 1966 that it was wrong to persecute someone simply because of their parentage, which would have saved more lives had he said it earlier. In January 1967, Mao ordered the army to support the Left, meaning the general aims of the Red Guards, although increasing factionalism among the revolutionaries meant that separate wings of the People's Liberation Army (PLA) might soon find themselves opening fire on each other in the name of differing interpretations of Mao's words. In February 1967, units of the PLA at last began a crackdown, leading to several incidents where the army stormed Red Guard enclaves. It had become another civil war, in all but name, but with everyone claiming to be loyalists. By July, the assaults reached the Party's summit. Liu Shaoqi himself, the supposed ruler of China and Mao's successor as Chairman, was dragged to an 'accusation meeting' and made to stand for two hours suffering harangues and beatings. His wife was forced to parade in the silk dress she had worn to a foreign diplomatic meeting. Aged sixty-nine, Liu resigned as head of state on 7 August 1967.

The following month, with Mao's main greatest rivals beaten into submission, forced to resign, or killed, Mao called for the factions to unite once more. This required the purging of 'ultra-Leftists', and the tide turned against some of the more radical Red Guards. They, along with thousands of others who were suspected of being in league with them, were killed or sent to labour camps for reform. Cannibalism returned, not to hold off starvation, but as a symbol of loyalty: there were reports of Party faithful in some areas being forced to eat the livers of class enemies. China was eating itself, at Mao's instigation.

Nixon in China

Mao was now an old man. His health faded as the deprivations of his youth and the excesses of his time in power caught up with him. He sometimes accepted a rub-down with a hot towel, but his occasional swims were the only time he saw anything approaching a bath. He did not even brush his teeth, preferring instead to rinse them with tea each morning. Considering the hardships he had undergone, it is remarkable he was still alive at all; he experienced some respiratory problems, and, if his doctor's memoirs are to be believed, suffered an outbreak of venereal disease that he managed to pass on to several of his concubines. 'I wash myself', he once boasted, 'inside the bodies of my women', referring to the succession of attractive, politically vetted nurses, dance companions, and secretaries who kept him company in his office and in bed.

Although the Party and the army were at least nominally back under control, the restless youth of China still stood little chance of finding work. Things had been bad enough before 1968, but the Cultural Revolution had forced down industrial production and destroyed many places of employment. Mao expanded the programme sending urban unemployed to work in the fields. Millions of young people, intellectuals in need of 're-education', and Party officials whose revolutionary resolve was found to be lacking were relocated. Since moving mouths from starving cities to equally hungry peasant villages would be unwelcome, many of them ended up in inhospitable border regions, on farms set up by the army.

In October 1968, the 12th Plenum of the Central Committee of the Chinese Communist Party met in Beijing. Less than a third of the original members were left, and Mao had to appoint ten new ones in order to achieve a quorum of fifty. Liu Shaoqi was tried for a long list of supposed crimes against the Party, some stretching back over forty years. Most of the evidence against him was obtained through torture.

Satisfied that China's internal problems were resolved, Mao turned his attentions abroad. The new Russian leader Leonid Brezhnev had started to undo some of the reforms instituted by Khrushchev. With a clampdown in Czechoslovakia, Brezhnev asserted Russia's right to invade other Communist nations where their behaviour threatened the cause of world Communism. This was aimed at dissenting Warsaw Pact countries in Eastern Europe, but Mao interpreted it as a threat to China.

His response, unstated, of course, was to court the US. If Mao could cultivate some form of friendship with the Americans, this would surely dissuade the Russians from any attempt to invade China. Mao deliberately provoked an international incident by sending 300 Chinese troops to occupy the disputed island of Zhenbao on the Sino-Soviet border in March 1969. The Russians played into his hands, opening fire on a decoy party only to find themselves in the midst of a Chinese ambush. The Chinese were beaten back with thirty casualties, and suffered ten times as many in a second skirmish two weeks later. Sixty Russians were left dead or wounded.

The border clashes got America's attention. In July, restrictions on US citizens travelling to China were lifted and China responded with an olive branch of its own. Two American sailors who had inadvertently entered Chinese waters a few days earlier were repatriated without fuss – previously, they would have been paraded as suspected spies.

Mao's desire for more normal Sino-American relations was shared by the US president, Richard Nixon. Nixon was a fervent anti-Communist, but he sought rapprochement with Mao because it was ridiculous to keep pretending that Nationalist Taiwan spoke for all China.

Lin Biao was the latest of Mao's recognised successors. This was partly because he helped fire the Cultural Revolution with the Little Red Book, but also because he was instrumental in quelling it. Large parts of China were only restored to order through martial law. Lin, however, was not an ideal choice. He seemed loyal to Mao, but he was a nervous, jumpy hypochondriac, given to eccentric behaviour and bouts of self-imposed isolation.

At the turn of the 1970s, some acquaintances of Lin's became embroiled in factional in-fighting with other Party members, and Mao began to doubt his choice of successor. This, of course, had other implications, since falling out of favour with Mao was not a simple matter of demotion or early retirement. If Lin lost Mao's support, he was liable to become a victim of the next round of purges, and suffer a fate like that of Liu Shaoqi. Lin's son, Liguo, grew concerned about what might happen after Mao's death, and as his father's position become further eroded, he commenced a secret plot called Project 571, supposedly because in Chinese, 571 (*wu qi yi*) was a homonym for 'armed uprising'. However, considering the customary unimaginative ciphers of Communist terminology, it may have originally referred to a planned commencement date in May 1971.

Little came of Project 571 – Lin was probably unaware, at least in the early stages, of his son's plans, although he continued to court disaster by snubbing Mao at public occasions, turning up late or under duress. Lin's claims of ill health grew increasingly frequent, and he only attended the May Day parade after a dressing down from Zhou Enlai. Ironically, by September, Mao was convinced that Lin was up to something, and the two squabbled over who should be head of state – not because they coveted the post, but because they didn't. The role comprised little more than ceremonial duties that would deprive its incumbent of the chance to hold positions involving real power.

For his part, Lin Biao carried on obliviously. His main concern in the early days of September 1971 was the planning of his daughter's wedding. But even as Mao began to move towards officially removing Lin Biao from office, Lin Liguo and his associates debated the ideal scheme to kill off their leader. From straightforward gunmen, their plans advanced to flamethrowers. Eventually, it was suggested that, since Mao was unlikely to put himself near to anything that might 'accidentally' kill him, the best option would be to rig an anti-aircraft gun so it could aim low enough to blow him and his bodyguards away. None of the plans made it beyond the conversational stage. For the son of a general, Liguo demonstrated little aptitude for planning or preparation.

Convinced that Mao was about to order Lin Biao's arrest, Lin Liguo commandeered a military plane, flew it to Beijing, and bundled his father and other family members onboard. Informed that he could be under threat, Lin Biao, it seems reluctantly, agreed to fly to Guangzhou, where he could debate his next move – a challenge to Mao's authority, perhaps. But on hearing that a plane was preparing to take Lin away, a suspicious Zhou Enlai ordered it to stay on the ground. Given no choice but to wait or flee, the Lin family plane bolted down the unlit runway and made a dash for Mongolia.

It never reached its destination, and an official report later concluded that it ran out of fuel, its nine occupants killed in a fire that ensued when it tried to make an emergency landing. Whether the plane really ran out of fuel, whether it crashed, landed, or was shot down, and whether Lin Biao died, survived, or was even on board, are all still open to debate. He was certainly never seen again, and his disappearance was spun as the aftermath of a failed coup attempt.

Although he had come through unscathed, Mao appeared to have been betrayed by the very man he had groomed to succeed him. He spent two months in deep depression, and began to suffer the after-effects of congestive heart failure. He drank against his doctor's advice, and evaded specialist medical examinations, forcing doctors to conduct them with minimal equipment in his office. When he attended a funeral early in 1972, he had visibly aged.

Things were going better, at least, in his dealings with America. In 1970, Edgar Snow, who had made Mao internationally famous with *Red Star Over China*, visited Beijing. He and his wife were the first foreigners permitted to stand at Mao's side during the celebration of the foundation of the People's Republic – a message to other 'American friends' that was too subtle for American diplomats to spot.

China made a more obvious gesture in March 1971. The first Chinese sports team to play abroad since the Cultural Revolution was the table-tennis squad at the World Championships that month in Nagoya, Japan. Glenn Cowan, a young player on the American team, was heard to say that he would like to visit China one day, and the news was immediately relayed to Mao. After discussion with Zhou Enlai, Mao decided this was too vague as a basis for any action, but he apparently had a change of heart that night. Drifting off to sleep, under the influence of his customary sedatives, he mumbled to his nurse that he was going to invite the whole US team.

Barely three months after the American table-tennis players were feted in Beijing, a far more clandestine visit took place. Nixon's National Security Advisor Henry Kissinger faked an illness in Pakistan, allowing him to sneak on a plane to China without the attention of the world's media. He returned more publicly later in the year, in order to arrange a visit of great diplomatic weight. The President of the United States, Richard Nixon himself, was coming to China.

Kissinger negotiated a joint statement by the Americans and Chinese which proclaimed their shared desire to contain Russian expansion. Only Taiwan remained a contentious issue. America had supported Chiang Kai-shek's 'Republic of China' for decades, and would not allow a Communist invasion. America had, however, recalled the two navy destroyers that symbolically patrolled the Taiwan Strait. The eventual Shanghai Communiqué found a diplomatic way around the stumbling block. America made a statement with which not even Chiang Kai-shek would argue, saying that there was only one China, and that Taiwan was part of it. How the Communists and Nationalists dealt with this would be up to them, and so long as they dealt with it peacefully, America would not interfere.

Nixon arrived in February 1972. His official intention was to hold a series of talks with Zhou Enlai, who had been China's Premier since 1949. But to many in China, and to the world at large, Mao was still the real leader. A 'courtesy call' on Mao was therefore a vital element of Nixon's schedule. By now, Mao was very frail. Bedridden for months, he forced himself to exercise so he would be able to make simple movements such as getting out of a chair, in order to create a good impression.

'People like me', he told Nixon, 'sound a lot like big cannons. For example, [we say] things like "the whole world should unite and defeat imperialism ...'" Mao and Zhou Enlai then laughed. To an American like Nixon, this was a sign of self-deprecating humour; to an oriental mind, it was a sign of uneasy embarrassment. The younger Mao might have seen talking to America as a necessary evil, akin to his brief flirtation with the Nationalists in his youth, an exploitation of 'useful idiots' to further the cause of world Communism. Perhaps this older Mao still felt the same, but to all involved, he seemed to be accepting China's role on the world stage, as a large and responsible nation which could not secretly instigate revolutions abroad.

As Mao's health continued to deteriorate, he was torn by contradictory impulses. Part of him remained the youthful idealist, determined to exist in a state of constant revolution, continuing to call for sweeping measures like the Hundred Flowers or further Great Leaps, determined to whip China along the path to a socialist utopia. But he was also a tired old man, who acknowledged that China, like him, could do with a rest. With Lin Biao dead and no obvious heir-apparent, Mao found himself rehabilitating some of the Party members he had purged. By the time Zhou Enlai was hospitalised with terminal cancer, the country was in the hands of the relatively young Wang Hongwen, who had risen through the ranks as a result of the Cultural Revolution, and Deng Xiaoping, once purged on suspicion of wanting to reintroduce capitalism. By 1974, Mao's decline was impossible to ignore. Cataracts had rendered him almost blind, and he required a secret supply of oxygen in his state limousine to make the journey to public meetings. His nurse, Zhang Yufeng, held a position of great influence, simply because she read Party documents to him, and because she was the only one who could understand his slurred responses. Mao had developed bedsores, and his lungs were suffering the predictable effects of a lifetime of smoking. He had also developed Lou Gehrig's disease, an affliction that would eventually paralyse his throat and respiratory system. His doctor gave him two more years, at best.

Even as he began to die, Mao fought to steer the Chinese state. Wang Hongwen formed a quiet faction with Mao's estranged wife Jiang Qing that met with Mao's disapproval. Accordingly, Mao shunted him aside, promoting Deng Xiaoping to a position that would eventually make him the leader of China after Mao's death. Even then Mao dithered, wondering whether the former Hunan First Secretary Hua Guofeng might actually be a better choice.

In February 1976, Mao welcomed in the Chinese New Year in the lonely company of his nurse, being spoon-fed mashed food because it was all he could eat. Realising that the end was near, his Party colleagues began to scheme furiously, and Deng Xiaoping was reprimanded for 'allowing' demonstrations that supported him. Mao suffered a heart attack, but soon displayed a sign of his old bullishness when he refused to sanction a call for foreign aid after an earthquake in Tangshan – many lives could have been saved if he had.

In June he summoned some of his closest associates to his bedside, including Jiang Qing, whom he detested so much that her former bedside vigils had been conducted behind him, so he would not see her. He said that he had achieved two great things in his life. One was winning the war against Chiang Kai-shek that had driven the Nationalists off mainland China and led to the foundation of the People's Republic. The other was the Cultural Revolution, which, Mao was convinced, still had yet to run its course. Mao issued a stern warning to his successors that there would be more bloodshed if they did not handle the after-effects properly. 'Heaven alone knows what you will do', he said.[1]

Mao suffered another heart attack on 2 September. He died in the early minutes of 9 September. His last words, spoken to his nurse earlier that evening, were, 'I feel very ill. Call the doctors.'[2]

The Heart of Tiananmen

Mao had clearly expressed a wish to be cremated. 'We should all be burnt after we die,' he wrote, 'turned into ashes and used for fertiliser.'[1] His preference was roundly ignored by the authorities, who dispatched a team of embalmers to somehow preserve the body. The plan was to create an iconic leader lying forever in state, in imitation of Lenin in Moscow's Red Square, but pride forbade the Chinese from asking the Soviets for help. Instead, the embalmers got to work, trying to keep the temperature of the body down and improvising with a number of untried and experimental methods.

'The results were shocking,' wrote Mao's physician Li Zhisui, who had pleaded with them that the embalming plans were unrealistic.

> Mao's face was bloated, as round as a ball, and his neck was now the width of his head. This skin was shiny, and the formaldehyde oozed from his pores like perspiration. His ears were swollen, too, sticking out from his head at right angles. The corpse was grotesque.[2]

Li's account of Mao's death and its aftermath is a textbook warning to history about the dangers of dictatorship. The dying leader is pressed to initial a document anointing his successor, although it is not clear he knows what he is signing. Power factions leap into action, keen to associate themselves with the pious preservation of their leader's remains, until the process looks ready to fail. At that point, they scramble to distance themselves from the project, hoping someone else will take the blame. Briefly, Dr Li fears that as the Chairman's physician, he will be accused of murdering him, or pilloried for refusing to adopt some of the cronies' more far-fetched suggested cures, such as feeding the dying Chairman powdered pearls.

Eventually, the body of the Chairman would be installed in its permanent place of rest, a mausoleum that remains the sole building on the plaza at Tiananmen Square. The building's very construction was a performance of national mourning, overseen by a committee from China's far-flung provinces and subject to acts of 'symbolic voluntary labour' by 700,000 people. Its materials were a veritable travelogue of China, with granite from Sichuan, quartz from the Kunlun Mountains, rocks pointedly hewn from the Chinese side of Mount Everest, and lumber from the site of his Jiangxi Soviet.

His body, or what's left of it, remains there to this day, as patriotic visitors line up around the edge of the square for the privilege of being marched past for a brief five seconds. Only his head is visible, and that looks suspiciously waxy; the body itself is hidden beneath a hammer-and-sickle flag.

Security is intensely high. It is not enough to have passed through the bag scanners of the metro. One is scanned once more to enter the underpass to the square, and one's bags

Mao's mausoleum in Tiananmen Square.

are scanned yet again before they are shoved into lockers. The visitor is then scanned yet again, and their ID checked, before they are permitted inside to dash around the Chairman at a respectable distance. It is, however, possible for a small two-year-old child to squeeze through the railings into the mausoleum yard, at which point the response time for the People's Liberation Army guards brings them to the scene in just over two seconds. I know this because my son Alexander undertook this experiment on his own initiative in December 2012. The People's Liberation Army was very nice about it.

The successful honouring of the departed Chairman was one of the factors that most animated his would-be successors. The mausoleum as it stands today is the final result of multiple spats and arguments, several falls from grace, an absolutely pointless argument about whether his alabaster statue should sit with its legs crossed, and the aforementioned drama about whether it would even be possible to preserve his corpse at all. Even as they fought over his remains, battle lines were drawn over the succession.

Within a month of Mao's death, the ringleaders of the Cultural Revolution – the so-called 'Gang of Four' – were rounded up and arrested. Mao's wife Jiang Qing, the propaganda official Zhang Chunqiao, Mao's sometime successor Wang Hongwen, and Yao Wenyuan, the man who had written the infamous critique of *Hai Rui Dismissed from Office*, were detained on suspicion of 'anti-socialist activities' and imprisoned. All but Yao died in jail, Jiang Qing by her own hand in 1991.

The new Chairman and Premier, Hua Guofeng, briefly pursued a policy of the 'Two Whatevers', outlined in a newspaper article in February 1977:

> We will resolutely uphold whatever policy decisions Chairman Mao made, and unswervingly follow whatever instructions Chairman Mao gave.[3]

For Hua and his fellow 'Whateverists', this was a loyal and dutiful adherence to the wishes of the departed leader. For many other factions it was a ridiculously blind and dogmatic, perhaps even *religious* fanaticism that blatantly ignored changes in both domestic and international circumstances. Mao's old guard was dying off at much the same time as him, leaving political appointees who had somehow weathered the storms of the past two decades, facing rivals who had suffered at their hands. Among several contending factions, the one that eventually scrambled to the top was drawn from rehabilitated victims of the Cultural Revolution, a resurgence of frankly anti-Mao interest.[4]

Mao's long-term inheritor was a man who had formerly been the victim of some of his anti-Rightist campaigns. Deng Xiaoping (1904–97) had been one of the Returning Students who fast-tracked into Party positions after indoctrination in Soviet Russia. He had been a supporter of the young Mao in several Party spats, and indeed had been demoted for Maoist leanings, only to be re-promoted after Mao's bounce back to power at the Zunyi Conference. Although he had once been an enforcer for Mao's Anti-Rightist programmes in the early days of the People's Republic, he was purged during the Cultural Revolution for what, for Mao, was a worrying interest in taking the 'capitalist road', which would have wiped out Mao's planned reforms.

Deng's policy might be best described as an elaborate game of 'What would Chairman Mao do?'. He seized upon one of Mao's statements about 'seeking the truth from facts', and argued that since the facts of geopolitics and economics had changed, it was a noble and truly Maoist act to change with the times. The first obvious implementation of this policy came in September 1977, when he proclaimed that it was time for China to 'eliminate chaos and return to normal' (*boluan fanzheng*).

The statement was controversial for many factions. For the Whateverists, it strongly implied that the previous

Deng Xiaoping, who undid many of Mao's policies in the guise of following them.

years had been *abnormal*, and that a mistaken path was now being *corrected*. For younger reformers, it ultimately would not go far enough in pursuing the architects of Mao's atrocities, leaving far too many of his cronies unharmed or quietly allowed to retire. Regardless, Deng somehow had the numbers and the leverage to mount a challenge to the Whateverists, and Hua Guofeng's time as Premier and Chairman was short-lived. Deng, however, did not seize those positions for himself. Although history widely recognises him as China's paramount leader throughout the 1980s, he often allowed others to take the political roles in the spotlight. Premiers, in particular, would come and go, but Deng remained the true power behind the throne. In one of his most diplomatic gestures, he carefully parsed human failings in quasi-scientific terms, suggesting that if someone was '70% good' and only '30% bad', then they still fell on the right side of their statistics. This entirely made-up qualification, which was itself a quote from Mao that originally referred to Stalin, has been oft-cited in the years since as some sort of defence, writing off Mao's worse failures as if they were rounding errors in accounts, and not the deaths of millions.[5] But Deng's commentary was not aimed specifically at Mao, but at an entire generation of senior officials welcomed back into government after an underhand purge of revolutionaries unsuited to run a country.[6]

Not that Deng ever put it in those terms, but his long decade in power would indeed amount to a course-correction, rejecting Mao's 'permanent revolution' and transforming China into a modern nation-state. Deng couched his reforms in terms that would be recognised and understood by the many Party officials who had taken the chance, post-Mao, to visit foreign countries, and who had returned astounded by the degree to which the Chinese had been swindled.

'Recently,' he said, 'our comrades had a look abroad. The more we see, the more we realise how backward we are.'[7] His answer for them was the 'Four Modernisations': reforms to agriculture, industry, defence, and science/technology that had previously been proposed by the late Zhou Enlai. Much of his planned reforms cloaked a slow return to capitalist principles, at first cautiously phrased as a desire for a 'moderately prosperous society' (*xiaokang*). Some people, he warned, would get rich first, but everybody else would get their chance.[8]

Deng, like all the Chinese leaders after him, had to contend with the fact that the People's Republic only possessed a single ruling organisation. While there were several squib parties within the government of the People's Republic, they have only ever functioned as rubber-stamps for the Communist Party's decisions – effectively, the People's Republic is a one-party state, which means it lacks any sense of a 'loyal opposition' that can be relied upon to propose new ideas or fight unpopular decisions. Instead, all decisions, all changes and about-faces, all innovations, need to be parsed as if they are part of an ongoing, never-retreating march towards utopia.

One such reversal of Mao's projects came in 1979 with the promulgation of a Family Planning Policy that limited, instead of encouraging, the rapid growth of the Chinese population. The legislation is remembered today by its nickname, the 'One-Child Policy', because for the Han-ethnicity Chinese majority, that was largely what it meant. Loopholes allowed for ethnic minorities to have more children and, soon, waivers were often granted to Chinese families whose one child inconveniently turned out to be a girl. Despite the bold claims of the Chinese marriage law and Mao's utopia, boys were still regarded as somehow worth more, particularly because so many families clung to the superstition that male heirs were required to continue ritual ceremonies to the ancestors. All of this ran contrary to the atheist, fiercely egalitarian policies of Chinese officialdom, but nevertheless, for the next generation, China's families would be subject to censure, fines, and even compulsory abortions if they dared to defy the rules. As Deng gently began to turn China towards a capitalist economy, this often served to concentrate the meagre wealth of four grandparents and two parents into a single child – a new generation of 'Little Emperors' shouldering the burden of all their parents' dreams and educational expectations.

America finally accorded the People's Republic diplomatic recognition in 1979, an act which left the *Republic* of China on Taiwan in political limbo. Since there could only be 'one China', and the international community now recognised the People's Republic, there was no space for Taiwan in many international councils, committees, or bodies. China's seat on the United Nations Security Council was forfeited to Beijing, and Taiwan ever since has had to play delicate games of political brinkmanship over its quasi-independent, quasi-rebel status.[9]

Deng, for his part, regarded this as a problem that could be turned to his advantage, expressing his hope that Taiwan would look to the Chinese mainland and come to understand that a voluntary return to China was desirable. In this policy, he hoped that his attitude towards Hong Kong would prove to be an example that set the Taiwanese people's minds at ease, as he had a plan that he hoped would bring Hong Kong back into China, too.

Deng's reforms ushered in meteoric economic growth: a boom-time in prosperity that made some people fortunes, but ruined others who were unable to adapt from the old 'iron rice bowl' days of guaranteed Party support. Far in the south, Deng initiated a series of Special Economic Zones, largely concentrated around Hong Kong, as satellite factory-towns to supply foreign business interests over the border. In the most famous example, the sleepy fishing town of Shenzhen, with a population of 30,000 in 1980, mushroomed to an industrial metropolis of 17.5 million people today. Such Special Economic Zones became prime movers of China's new economy, pouring foreign wealth into the country.

In the late 1980s, Soviet Russia underwent its period of *perestroika*, a restructuring of hardline values that eventually led to a counter-revolution and the dismantling of Communism. The idea met with some support among young Chinese students, leading to a multi-factional sit-in on Tiananmen Square itself, overseen by young Chinese activists calling for a Fifth Modernisation: democracy. Such protests arose at the end of many years of economic reforms that had only worked for some, and a precipitous decline in the enrolments of young members of the Communist Party.[10] The youth of China, it seemed, were ready to tell the Communist Party that it no longer spoke for them, and did so in that historically famous place of assembly: the area in front of the Gate of Heavenly Peace in Beijing.

In May 1989, students from the Central Academy of Fine

The modern metropolis of Shenzhen, as envisioned by Deng Xiaoping.

Arts demonstrated that they had internalised many of the ideas and tactics of Mao-era propaganda. Over the course of four days, they erected a ten-metre statue in foam and rubber, the 'Goddess of Democracy'. Most photography of this short-lived icon favours the icon itself, picturing her face-on, a torch held high like New York's Statue of Liberty. But it was the placement of the Goddess of Democracy that was most worthy of notice – rare images taken from behind the statue show that it was sited directly across from the portrait of Mao that graces the front of the Gate of Heavenly Peace. She was not merely holding a loft a light of enlightenment; she was brandishing a torch in defiance in the face of the Chairman himself.

The Tiananmen Square protest was one of several grassroots movements that sprang up around China in 1989. Jiang Zemin, then the mayor of Shanghai, cautioned that such protesters were effectively denying the nobility of the

The original Goddess of Democracy was destroyed, but there are copies all over the world.

revolution, offering the dangerous notion that the forward-march of Marxist history could be reversed or revised. The Chinese Communist Party was the true and final saviour of the Chinese people, and its policies were always to be regarded as further steps towards the ultimate good. To even suggest otherwise amounted to 'historical nihilism' (*lishixuwu-zhuyi*).

Such people could not be allowed to challenge the Party's authority, even as the Party seemingly dismantled so much of its own previous infrastructure and beliefs. In June 1989, Deng Xiaoping waited until the visiting Russian leader Mikhail Gorbachev had left China before he sent tanks to crush the demonstrations.

Strike Black, Sing Red

Deng Xiaoping, whom Mao always suspected of capitalist leanings, allowed increasing incursions of a capitalist economy into China. With over a billion inhabitants, 'Communist' China is now the single largest market for capitalist products in the world, an engine that can make or break investments from abroad. The media are apt to report the glittering successes of the successful oligarchs, with their foreign educations and their Ferraris, but Deng's rationalisation of the economy was also a period of drastic, cataclysmic change. Sixty million workers were laid off from state-owned industries in the 1990s. Some of them, true enough, took the plunge (literally *xiahai*, 'jump into the sea') and became entrepreneurs.[1] Others ended up on the scrap heap. Some became rich by ransacking the ruins of Mao's Third Front initiative, now quietly shut down after the thaw in international relations. Secret factory plants once built for tank parts and artillery shells were suddenly acquired at knock-down prices and retooled to make tractors and fridges. Down in the Southern Economic Zone, thriving industrial concerns funnelled car parts and zippers, crockery and sofas across the border into Hong Kong and out to the world – although the fact that Hong Kong was not 'Chinese' was beginning to rankle.

During the revolution, Mao had defiantly revoked any treaty made by former Chinese governments. One might be forgiven, then, for imagining that whatever state China's borders were in on the date of his proclamation in 1949 would now be set in perpetuity. Ironically, it was capitalism itself that led to the reversal of this implied policy, as estate agents and bankers in Hong Kong began to question the validity of mortgages that extended past the year 1997.

While the *island* of Hong Kong was supposedly ceded to Britain in perpetuity at the end of the Opium Wars, the colony's New Territories were only granted to the British as a ninety-nine-year *lease* several decades later in 1898. Would the Chinese be expecting to get the New Territories back, and if they did, how could the colony expect to survive when deprived of 82 per cent of its land area, including much of the vital power plants and reservoirs?

Imperial treaties or not, the People's Republic wanted Hong Kong back. The Chinese regarded this as a restoration of Chinese territory, but many in Hong Kong felt betrayed by the British. In an attempt to mollify the Hong Kong Chinese, the PRC issued a Basic Law for the former colony, making it a Special Administrative Region until 2047. This was designed to please all parties. The Chinese would ultimately get Hong Kong. The British and Hong Kong Chinese knew a lot could happen in five decades – it was, after all, only that long since the foundation of the People's Republic itself.

Mao himself recognised that, if left unsupervised, the revolution could stall within three generations, causing China to revert to a capitalist economy, undoing much of what he had fought to achieve. Mao meant this as a warning. For the capitalist West, it was a hope. In 2001, China joined the World Trade Organisation. In 2002, private entrepreneurs were permitted to join the Communist Party.

As China 'opened up' following the death of Mao, tourism had been one of the first topics on the mind of the Deng Xiaoping, who had his beady eye on the potential of a permanently renewable resource of hard currency. 'If each foreign tourist would spend $1000 in China,' he argued, 'with a total of 10 million tourists visiting China every year, China could earn $10 billion.'[2] But Deng's vision, of course, was intended for a more traditional form of leisure travel, such as the Great Wall (which was soon opened to visitors on multiple locations), the Terracotta Army, or the Forbidden City.

Official endorsement of tourism as a patriotic and educational *Party* phenomenon would not come until 1991, two years after the Tiananmen Square protests caused the authorities to question if modern youth was on-message. Among several re-education initiatives, the school curriculum was transformed to emphasise Chinese history not in terms of class struggle, but of a story with a happy ending as Mao and his Party came to the rescue. A Patriotic Education Campaign suggested that the young visit sites of *Communist* historical interest, and a vast series of projects began to create enough of them to go around. In a sense, it encapsulated a generational conflict, not only over a young China that had not experienced the formative conflicts of the Revolution, but of the 'Little Emperors' born after the instigation of the One-Child Policy, regarded by some sectors as snooty snowflakes with no recollection of true hardship. In 1996, a magazine coined a term for such patriotic travels: Red Tourism (*hongse lüyou*).[3]

Yan'an, the site of Mao's 1930s guerrilla resistance, was once favoured *because* it was remote, inhospitable, and inaccessible. Now it is a mecca of Red Tourism, blessed by ultra-modern transport links – just two and a half hours from Xi'an by bullet train – where the economic impact of leisure travel has outstripped agriculture in the local economy. Now it is the site of 'Golden Yan'an', a new 'old' town built on expropriated farmland, and offering employment to the former farmers by getting them to dress up in a multi-faceted Chinese history experience.

'History', however, is something of a flexible subject in modern China. It is, it seems, whatever the Party says it is, and anyone who quibbles with it is accused of 'historical nihilism'. Whereas most historians worldwide consider it their duty to question an established narrative, and to investigate new interpretations of data, today such enquiry is strongly discouraged.

Today, there is a new narrative, repeatedly presented to the public as if it has always been there, in which the paramount leader Xi Jinping is presented as Mao's just and noble successor. His father, Xi Zhongxun, a frankly faceless Party grandee in the twentieth century, has been reframed as one of the prime movers of both the Revolution and its reform, and even as the man who came up with the idea for the Special Economic Zones in the 1980s. This is not to say that Xi Zhongxun was *not* a significant revolutionary figure, a military leader, and an efficient politician – merely that I managed to make it through several college-level histories of China in the 1990s without once hearing or reading his name.

I have resisted the temptation with the updated edition of this book to do what so many Chinese historians have done over the last few years: sneaking him into key moments in earlier chapters such as meetings at Yan'an, a chat with the Dalai Lama, being denounced in the Cultural Revolution and rehabilitated in time for the economic reforms. The student of history might observe the interesting philosophical conundrum that this presents – all these things *did* happen, but almost nobody seemed to think they were worth mentioning until recently. Since his death in 2002, he has migrated from the footnotes to the main story, all because his son, Xi Jinping, happens to have become the paramount leader of China.

There is a certain advantage to a degree of political anonymity. You can't be attacked if nobody knows who you are. Xi Jinping certainly learned that the hard way during the Cultural Revolution, for which his teens and early twenties were spent living in a cave in Yan'an, from which he submitted ten unsuccessful applications to the Communist Party before he was finally allowed in.

Thereafter he climbed through the ranks, finishing the 1970s catching up with his lost education and earning a degree in chemical engineering. He became a Party member after graduation, and was soon shunted sideways from what seemed to be a promising career in agricultural technology to become the vice-mayor of Xiamen, one of the Special Economic Zones, in 1985. It was another sixteen years before he became the governor of the whole province, and was thence shunted into numerous prominent positions that made it clear he was being groomed for the top spot.

His main rival was Bo Xilai, the charismatic son of another of Deng Xiaoping's inner circle, a history major who had risen to become the mayor of Dalian, and then the mega-city of Chongqing. Bo was brought down in 2012 by a jackpot of scandals, the biggest of which was the involvement of his wife in the murder of a British businessman. Had the Bo family not fallen so spectacularly from grace, it might have been *his* father that I was writing about here.

Nevertheless, both men were 'princelings' of some form or other – privileged inheritors of the very same 'aristocracy' about which Mao had once issued dire warnings. In order to make it clear to the public that they were not mere beneficiaries of nepotism, both men needed to signify that they were ideological successors to Mao himself. In the case of Bo Xilai, he signified his Party affiliations with a campaign that recalled Mao's heyday. He suggested the patriotic rehabilitation of many of the good old Party songs of old, insisting that Chongqing radio play revolutionary songs instead of today's pop hits. He inaugurated a propaganda-based singing contest and presided over the release of thirty-six new 'red songs' in the style of the old classics. He married this to a prolonged campaign against corrupt elements in administration and society. He called the entire process 'Strike Black, Sing Red'.[4]

As the contenders for the leadership duked it out in the media, both the victorious Xi Jinping and the vanquished Bo Xilai leaned heavily into Maoist imagery – pushing the songs of the good old days and the degree to which they could be seen as inheritors and re-interpreters of Mao's legacy. Both took their cues from the artful sophistry of Deng Xiaoping, whose policy of 'seeking truth from facts' effectively claimed to have been instituting reforms that Mao himself would surely have approved, if only he were alive and able to see the necessary data. Times, went the argument, were always changing – only the monolithic, iconic sight of Mao's face remained to unite the Chinese in their endeavours.

For anyone reared during the era of Deng Xiaoping, Xi might seem to be a revisionist. He claimed precisely the opposite, noting that his policies and proclamations were designed to correct and finesse policy decisions from the four decades since the death of Mao. He repeatedly alludes, for example, to the oft-forgotten second part of Deng Xiaoping's famous exhortation: 'Let some get rich first *for the purpose of achieving common prosperity faster*.' While early twenty-first-century observers hoped that the opening up of China would lead to liberalisation, free markets, and even democracy, Xi arrived to remind them that even economic prosperity was merely a means to an end – the creation of Mao's self-sufficient, wealthy utopia, what Xi calls the 'China Dream'.[5]

Xi Jinping Thought now has its own shelf in the libraries, but much of it is framed as a respectful reconsideration of

'The China Dream: A Strong Military.' Propaganda image, 2024.

Mao. 'Only socialism can save China,' said Xi in his centenary address to the Party. 'Only socialism can develop China.'[6]

China under Xi has also embraced many elements of a highly regulated surveillance society, of which Mao would have surely approved. Surely the Great Helmsman would have absolutely loved the digitisation of much of China's economy? When I visit China today, the authorities can track my every movement through my phone purchases – they can see every transaction, from the coffee I bought at Guangzhou station, to the metro I took to Foshan, to the noodles I had for lunch. If I were assembling a petrol bomb or going to a dissident rally, they might even know about it before I did. My money is merely a drop in the churning ocean of Chinese economics, but since 2020 Xi has pushed for a form of economic autarky: a decreased reliance on overseas trade and investment, in favour of 'internal circulation'.

Whereas the legacies of other Communist leaders like

Stalin and Khrushchev have been reconsidered by their successors, Xi has spent his entire term in office urging the Party faithful to honour Mao as the symbolic lodestone of the Party. In a speech in 2013, he said:

> Why did the Soviet Union disintegrate? An important reason was that ... the Soviet Union completely denied its history, the history of the Communist Party, Lenin, and Stalin, and created historical nihilism and confusing thinking. The Party was scattered, and the Soviet Union, an enormous socialist country, disintegrated. This is a cautionary tale![7]

Such a comment, however, turned out to be flexible on its definition of 'denial'. Xi would soon show that he was working within a framework summarised by a neo-Maoist as a careful redaction of history itself to serve the needs of the Party.

'For as long as the Cultural Revolution is a catastrophe in human history,' wrote the author Hongliang Zhang, 'the system that produced this catastrophe is an evil system, and the party that caused the catastrophe is a sinful party; the nation that caused the catastrophe is an evil nation.'[8]

The Cultural Revolution *was* a catastrophe. But the only way to solve this historiographical issue was to pretend that it wasn't, and to emphasise the many sacrifices and victories of the 70 per cent.

In the second decade of the twenty-first century, Xi

Jinping began to dismantle many of the checks and balances that had been installed to prevent someone from aping Mao's rise to power. The culmination came in 2018 when the Chinese legislature abolished term limits, effectively making Xi president for life with no clear successor. That same year, a new textbook published in Beijing for middle-school students described the Cultural Revolution not as the 'ten-year cataclysm' decried by Deng Xiaoping, but as a period of 'arduous exploration and development achievement.' Once again, history was being rewritten, and a nation already reluctant to discuss the truth of Mao's era was steering even further away from it.[9]

At a loose end in Shanghai in 2024, I dropped by the site of the First Congress of the Communist Party of China, a nondescript building at what used to be 106 Rue Wantz in the French Concession. A small museum inside chronicles the various individuals and events that literally got that Party started, although most of the Chinese visitors were more keen to have their photograph taken by the entirely everyday front door with its '106' nameplate.

I was more excited by the presence of a *bona fide* First Congress of the Communist Party of China gift shop, where I shopped in a frenzy for my First Congress of the Communist Party of China umbrella, my First Congress of the Communist Party of China pen, my First Congress of the Communist Party of China tote bags, and my First Congress of the Communist Party of China fridge magnet. There was even an *I've Been to the First Congress of the Communist Party of China* frame outside, where I had my photograph taken loaded with First Congress of the Communist Party of China swag.

I was but a single participant in a growing and, in some sense, relatively recent phenomenon, as the Communist Party attempts to merge the disparate disciplines of education, propaganda, national cohesion, and social harmony. Today, Red Tourism is a massive component of Chinese leisure travel, amounting to 540 million visits a year, or 20 per cent of all domestic Chinese tourism.[10] To put this in context, private investment in tourist experiences in Mao's old base at Yan'an has topped 50 *billion* yuan, ten times the amount spent to build Shanghai Disneyland.

Many of these sites are genuinely exciting, exulting in the undeniable achievement of modern China in catapulting itself into the twenty-first century, and the many heroic individuals who fought to throw off foreign invaders and social injustices. I have spent many years trying to drag fellow travellers along to see Changchun's Historical Museum for Japan's Occupation in North-East China, or the Zhuhai Martyrs' Cemetery. Such sites truly celebrate China's modern history in new and interesting ways, and are so much more informative to the jaded historian than *yet another temple*. But despite the earnest chronicles of heroism and sacrifice, there is something missing. At the Longhua Martyrs' Cemetery, built on the site of the Nationalists' execution ground in Shanghai, there are moving accounts of early heroes and revolutionaries, dioramas of battles, and accomplished oil paintings of crucial historical moments. Revolution, for the museum,

'Independence, Democracy', a sculpture by Ye Yushan at the Shanghai Martyrs' Cemetery.

is a state of grace towards which China groped during its 'Century of Humiliation', and then fought to maintain in the years that followed. There would be scope here, in a truly comprehensive installation, for an entire extra gallery about the Chinese who lost their lives in some of the wrong turns of the subsequent Chinese state, like the Great Leap Forward and the Cultural Revolution, but such discussions are characteristically muted.

Instead, the Longhua Martyrs' Cemetery favours the idea of revolutionary spirit as something that burned in the hearts of the characters whose stories are told in the exhibits, and should be nurtured and encouraged in everyone.

Pointing out that it presumably also flourished in at least some of the millions of people who were starved, beaten, or executed during Maoist purges and social experiments in the 1950s and 1960s would ruin the brilliantly told story of a past that marches ever onwards towards a utopian present.

*

Mao is an ironic icon, not just of the Communist Party, but of consumerism, his picture appearing on everything from blankets to wristwatches. Mao's personality clings on in images on the walls of Chinese classrooms and even, despite stern Party disapproval, among those of traditional gods on family altars.

He is also, of course, an icon of terror. In personal and public histories of the twentieth century, he has been blamed for the deaths of seventy million Chinese in famine and oppression. He epitomises the horror of the Cultural Revolution, and the hypocrisy of the Hundred Flowers Campaign and similar purges. But blaming Mao is easy. He might have said that political power grew from the barrel of the gun, but he did not pull every trigger. He did not administer every beating, or burn every book. In casting Mao as an all-powerful dictator who dominated China for twenty-seven brutal years, many of his opponents have merely put his personality cult to a new, but equally misleading use. It is, after all, easier to speak ill of the dead than it is to confront the uncountable atrocities of millions still living.

Bibliography and Further Reading

Nothing is certain with Mao. Facts have been twisted, garbled, and revised not only by his enemies and propagandists, but also by Mao himself. Stories he told foreign journalists in the 1930s, repeated for decades by dutiful biographers, have been found to be apocryphal or inaccurate. Youthful writings read by virtually no one, such as his call for the destruction of all books published since the Tang dynasty, have been later reprinted in mass-market editions, their relevance to their original time of publication blown all out of proportion. Even after his death, Mao periodically falls in and out of fashion.

The best all-round general biography is Philip Short's *Mao: A Life*, which delves in great detail into Mao's political manoeuvring within the Communist party, and follows his path to power. It faces serious competition from Jung Chang and Jon Halliday's highly readable *Mao: The Unknown Story*, which incorporates vast numbers of new Chinese sources and original interviews. However, these two landmark works occasionally differ on key points, and *The Unknown Story*, in its efforts to be sensational, sometimes merely refutes one piece of hearsay with another. It also grinds a personal axe that often makes it difficult to appreciate its broader achievement.

For Mao's own writings, the five-volume *Selected Works* should satisfy all but the most enthusiastic researchers. For those concentrating on the early years, Stuart Schram and Nancy Hodes's mammoth five-volume *Mao's Road to Power* offers an exhaustive selection. A more succinct anthology can be found in the single-volume *Selected Readings from the Works of Mao Tsetung*, published by Foreign Languages Press in 1971. Tellingly, it does not contain much from after 1957. Even his own compatriots seem to imply that he lost his touch after gaining power.

Stuart Schram's *The Thought of Mao Tsetung* offers a concise appraisal of Mao as a politician. Mao's failures are well chronicled in Jasper Becker's *Hungry Ghosts*, a terrifying account of the secret famine whose existence was unacknowledged until 1980. Meanwhile Lee Feigon's *Mao: A Reinterpretation* provocatively considers his role as a bogeyman and scapegoat. Feigon argues convincingly for Mao as a statesman, and notes that many of his *enemies* are responsible for the problems that China faces today.

For a first-hand glimpse of the tribulations, back-stabbing, and bitchiness that characterised the Long March and its aftermath, Otto Braun's memoir *A Comintern Agent in China* presents an enthralling account of the tense struggles both on the road and within the Party, particularly between the Russian-trained faction of which he was a member, and the home-grown, native Chinese Communists like Mao. I also recommend Hung Chang-tai's book *Mao's New World*, as a rare account of the days of celebration and enthusiasm for the Revolution, before its rhetoric was overwhelmed by the Great Leap Forward and the Cultural Revolution.

Li Zhisui's *The Private Life of Chairman Mao* is a

gripping chronicle of the latter half of Mao's life, written by someone who knew him intimately. Quan Yanchi's *Mao Zedong: Man, not God* is considerably thinner, but includes ghost-written anecdotes from Li Yinqiao, Mao's bodyguard for twenty years. This contains many interesting stories, along with much pro-Mao propaganda.

Mao's personality cult has obscured the vital role others played in the development and history of Chinese Communism. Gregor Benton's *Mountain Fires* and *New Fourth Army* reveal just some of these unsung stalwarts of the Communist struggle, men who fought the three-year guerrilla action that made the Long March possible, but who were marginalised from history simply because the future Chairman was not among their number.

In terms of the reassessment and, to some extent, resurgence of Mao in more recent times, *Chairman Mao's Children* by Xu Bin identifies the long tail of Mao's reign in terms of its psychological influence on both his inheritors and his adversaries. For anyone confused by the about-faces of the Deng Xiaoping era, and their implications today, I recommend Marquis and Qiao's *Mao and Markets*. *China's New Red Guards* by Jude Blanchette charts the rise of a new 'far left' in an increasingly capitalist China and appears increasingly prophetic as the era of Xi Jinping repurposes old-school Party ideology for the twenty-first century.

Becker, J. *Hungry Ghosts: China's Secret Famine* (London: 1996).

Benton, G. *Mountain Fires: The Red Army's Three-Year War in South China, 1934–1938* (Berkeley: 1992).

Benton, G. *New Fourth Army: Communist Resistance Along the Yangtze and the Huai, 1938–1941* (Berkeley: 1999).

Blanchette, J. *China's New Red Guards: The Return of Radicalism and the Rebirth of Mao Zedong* (New York: 2019).

Braun, O. *A Comintern Agent in China 1932–1939* (London: 1982).

Chang, J. and Jon Halliday. *Mao: The Unknown Story* (London: 2005).

Cheek, T. *Mao Zedong and China's Revolutions: A Brief History with Documents* (Boston: 2002).

Chen, T. *The Secret Listener: An Ingenue in Mao's Court* (New York: 2022).

Clark, P. *The Chinese Cultural Revolution: A History* (Cambridge: 2008).

Clements, J. *Confucius: A Biography* (Stroud: 2004).

Clements, J. *Pirate King: Coxinga and the Fall of the Ming Dynasty* (Stroud: 2004).

Clements, J. *The First Emperor of China* (Stroud: 2006).

Clements, J. *The Emperor's Feast: A History of China in Twelve Meals* (London: 2021).

Cosh, C. 'Why posting about egg-fried rice could land you in a Chinese jail' in *National Post* (9 November 2021).

Davin, D. *Mao* (Stroud: 1997).
Encyclopaedia Britannica (DVD Edition, 2002).
Dikötter, F. *Mao's Great Famine* (London: 2010).
Dirlik, A. 'Narrativizing Revolution: The Guangzhou Uprising (11–13 December 1927) in Workers' Perspective' in *Modern China*, Vol.23 No.24 (October 1997), pp. 363–97.
Engel, J. (ed.) *China Diary of George H. W. Bush: The Making of a Global President* (Princeton: 2008).
Esherick, J. *Reform and Revolution in China: The 1911 revolution in Hunan and Hubei* (Berkeley: 1976).
Feigon, L. *Mao: A Reinterpretation* (Chicago: 2002).
Fewsmith, J. *China Since Tiananmen: From Deng Xiaoping to Hu Jintao*, 2nd Edition (Cambridge: 2008).
Fontana, Dorothy Grouse. 'Background to the Fall of Hua Guofeng' in *Asian Survey*, Vol. 22 No.3 (March 1982), pp. 237–60.
Hung Chang-tai. *Mao's New World: Political Culture in the Early People's Republic* (Cornell University Press: 2011).
Kim San [Jang Jirak] and Nym Wales [Helen Foster Snow]. *Song of Ariran: The Life Story of a Korean Rebel* (New York: 1941).
Lee, L. and Sue Wiles. *Women of the Long March* (St Leonards: 1999).
Li, Z. *The Private Life of Chairman Mao: The memoirs of Mao's personal physician* [trans. Tai Hung-chao and Anne F. Thurston] (London: 1996).
Lin, C. *Red Tourism in China: Commodification of Propaganda* (London: 2022).

Macmillan, M. *Nixon and Mao: The Week that Changed the World* (New York: 2008).
Mao, Z. *Six Essays on Military Affairs* (Beijing: 1972).
Mao, Z. *Selected Readings from the Works of Mao Tsetung* (Beijing: 1971).
Mao, Z. *Selected Works* (Five volumes) (Beijing: 1977).
Marquis, C. and Qiao Kunyuan. *Mao and Markets: The Communist Roots of Chinese Enterprise* (New Haven: 2022).
Murck, A. (ed.) *Mao's Golden Mangoes and the Cultural Revolution* (Zurich: 2013).
Quan, Y. *Mao Zedong: Man, Not God* (Beijing: 1992).
Saich, T. *Finding Allies and Making Revolution: The Early Years of the Chinese Communist Party* (Leiden: 2020).
Schram, S. *Mao Tsetung* (Harmondsworth: 1957).
Schram, S. *Mao Tse-tung Unrehearsed: Talks and Letters 1956–1971* (Harmondsworth: 1974).
Schram, S. *The Thought of Mao Tsetung* (Cambridge: 1989).
Schram, S. *Foundations and Limits of State Power in China* (London: 1987).
Schram, S. & Nancy J. Hodes (eds). *Mao's Road to Power: Revolutionary Writings 1912–1949* (Five volumes) (Armony, NY: 1992).
Short, P. *Mao: A Life* (London: 2004).
Siao, Y. *Mao Tsetung and I Were Beggars* (New York: 1959).
Snow, E. *Red Star Over China* [revised edition] (Harmondsworth: 1972).

Snow, E. *Red Star Over China* (London: 1938).
Schram, S. *Mao Tsetung* (Harmondsworth: 1957).
Schram, S. *The Thought of Mao Tsetung* (Cambridge: 1989).
Schram, S. *Foundations and Limits of State Power in China* (London: 1987).
Spence, J. *Mao Zedong* (New York: 1999).
Sun, S. *The Long March* (London: 2006).
Tudda, C. *A Cold War Turning Point: Nixon and China 1969–72* (Baton Rouge: 2012).
Vogel, E. *Deng Xiaoping and the Transformation of China* (Cambridge, MA: 2011).
Xu, B. *Chairman Mao's Children: Generation and the Politics of Memory in China* (Cambridge: 2021).
Yang, J. *Tombstone: The Untold Story of Mao's Great Famine* (New York: 2012).
Yu, Y. *Socialism in China (1919–1965)* (Beijing: 2014).

Notes

Preface

1 Blanchette, *China's New Red Guards*, p. 5.

Early Life

1 Clements, *The Emperor's Feast*, p. 175. Mao's red braised pork was only developed in the 1950s after a tour of a soy sauce factory left the Great Helmsman queasy at unsanitary conditions, and demanding a dish that did not use the usual condiments.
2 Confucius, *Analects* XVII: 2.
3 Snow, *Red Star Over China*, p. 132.
4 Snow, *Red Star Over China*, p. 132.
5 E. Snow, *Red Star Over China* [revised edition] (Harmondsworth: 1972), p. 132.
6 P. Short, *Mao: A Life* (London: 2004) p. 30; J. Chang and Jon Halliday, *Mao: The Unknown Story*, (London: 2005) p. 7; the accounts differ considerably and there is little hope of verifying what actually happened.

The Republican Revolution

1 Snow, *Red Star* [rev. ed.], p. 158.
2 Snow, *Red Star* [rev. ed.], p. 161.
3 Short, *Mao,* p. 46.
4 Snow, *Red Star*, p. 166.
5 Short, *Mao*, pp. 64–5.
6 Snow, *Red Star* [rev. ed], p. 167.

The Thwarted Reformers

1 Snow, *Red Star* [rev. ed.] p. 167.
2 S. Schram and N. J. Hodes (eds), *Road to Power* 1 (Armony, NY: 1992), p. 61.
3 Schram and Hodes, *Road to Power* 1, p. 124.
4 Schram and Hodes, *Road to Power* 1, p. 94.
5 Schram and Hodes, *Road to Power* 1, pp. 73–4.
6 *Encyclopaedia Britannica*, 'Mao Zedong'.
7 Schram and Hodes, *Road to Power* 1, p. 389.

The Chinese Communist Party

1 Schram and Hodes, *Road to Power* 1, p. 526.
2 Schram and Hodes, *Road to Power* 2, p. 68.
3 Schram and Hodes, *Road to Power* 2, p. 125.
4 Short, *Mao,* p. 158.
5 Mao Zedong, 'Report on an Investigation of the Peasant Movement in Hunan', *Selected Readings from the Works of Mao Tsetung*, pp. 25–6, 29–30.

Maoism

1 Schram and Hodes, *Road to Power* 3, pp 30–31. Mao would repeat the phrase, or variants of it, on several later occasions, causing some confusion for later compilers of dictionaries of quotations.
2 Snow, *Red Star* [rev. ed.], p. 193.
3 Dirlik, 'Narrativizing Revolution', p. 363. I use the dual terms Canton Soviet and Guangzhou Commune to reflect both the dual identities of the city, and the fact that Zhang Tailei was a staunch admirer of the Paris Commune (1871), and framed his own revolt in similar terms.
4 Dirlik, 'Narrativizing Revolution', p. 379. Dirlik argues that local leadership should have borne much more of the blame for the mismanaged revolt – I think the evidence that he cites

continues to suggest that Zhang was a fervent and possibly naïve idealist, prepared to avoid the evidence in front of his own eyes that he would lack the necessary support, and to hence agree to the foreign adviser's ill-timed advice.

5 Kim and Wales, *Song of Ariran*, p. 92.

6 Dirlik, 'Narrativizing Revolution,' p. 385.

7 Kim and Wales, *Song of Ariran*, p. 101. Kim's posthumously published 1941 book, however, is misinformed about the ultimate fate of Zhang, falsely reporting that he died during the subsequent purges, five days after he had been killed at a roadblock. As local heroes, the leaders of the Guangzhou Uprising are celebrated today in a dozen statues that form the road to the Guangzhou Martyrs' Memorial Garden. The reliefs on the cenotaph above the mass grave depict rebels armed with little more than rocks and meat cleavers, and the brief moments of earnest celebration before the Canton Soviet was crushed.

8 Chang and Halliday, *Mao: The Unknown Story*, p. 58.

9 Schram and Hodes, *Road to Power* 3, p. 155; Mao, *Six Essays on Military Affairs*, pp. 36–8.

10 Schram and Hodes, *Road to Power* 3, p. 139.

The Long March

1 Chang and Halliday, *Mao*, p. 130. The girl reportedly died soon after, but He Zizhen conducted periodic searches for her for the rest of her life.

2 Short, *Mao*, p. 282, claims she was beheaded; Chang and Halliday, *Mao*, that she was shot.

3 Marquis and Qiao, *Mao and Markets*, p. 52.

4 Mao, 'Oppose Book Worship', *Selected Readings*, p. 42.

5 Schram and Hodes, *Road to Power* 4, pp. 820–1.

6 Schram and Hodes, *Road to Power* 4, p. 698.

7 Braun, *A Comintern Agent in China*, p. 39.

8 The location of the abandoned boy was known to Mao's brother,

who had supervised Xiao Mao's route into hiding, but he took it to his grave when he was killed in 1935. In 1952, He Zizhen believed she had found him, but the youth had already been claimed by another Party mother as her own. See Chang and Halliday, *Mao,* p. 130.

9 Braun, *A Comintern Agent in China*, p. 96.

10 See Chang and Halliday, *Mao*, p. 137.

The World at War

1 Snow, *Red Star*, p. 439.

2 Schram, *The Thought of Mao Tsetung*, pp. 113–14.

3 Schram, *Foundations and Limits of State Power in China*, p. 212.

Chairman Mao

1 Mao, *Selected Works* 4, pp. 411–23.

2 Mao, *Selected Works* 5, p. 19.

3 Short, *Mao*, p. 421.

4 Cosh, 'Why posting about egg-fried rice could land you in a Chinese jail.'

5 Hung, *Mao's New World*, p. 102.

One Hundred Flowers

1 Mao, *Selected Works* 5, p. 214.

2 Short, *Mao*, p. 455. Even in this, he was making a classical allusion, to a Tang dynasty poem.

3 Short, *Mao*, p. 457.

4 Short, *Mao*, p. 458.

5 Chang and Halliday, *Mao*, p. 435.

The Great Leap Forward

1 Chang and Halliday, *Mao*, pp. 457–8.

2 Chang and Halliday, *Mao*, p. 396.

3 S. Schram, *The Thought of Mao Tse-tung*, p. 195.

4 Short, *Mao*, p. 490.

The Cultural Revolution

1 Short, *Mao*, p. 513.
2 Schram, *Mao Tse-tung Unrehearsed: Talks and Letters 1956–1971*, p. 167.
3 Short, *Mao*, p. 513.
4 Marquis and Qiao, *Mao and Markets*, p. 68.
5 Marquis and Qiao, *Mao and Markets*, p. 237.

Nixon in China

1 Short, *Mao*, p. 625.
2 Chang and Halliday, *Mao*, p. 654.

The Heart of Tiananmen

1 Blanchette, *China's New Red Guards*, p. 24.
2 Li, *The Private Life of Chairman Mao*, p. 20.
3 Fontana, 'Background to the Fall of Hua Guofeng', p. 239.
4 Fontana, 'Background to the Fall of Hua Guofeng', pp. 239, 242. Fontana's descriptions of the forgotten factions forms a fascinating series of *what-ifs*, should history have played out only slightly differently.
5 Blanchette, *China's New Red Guards*, p. 36. It was not even part of Deng's 1981 'Resolution on Certain Questions on the History of Our Party', but was an off-hand comment in an interview given to an Italian journalist.
6 Vogel, *Deng Xiaoping and the Transformation of China*, pp. 698–9.
7 Vogel, *Deng Xiaoping and the Transformation of China*, p. 218.
8 Vogel, *Deng Xiaoping and the Transformation of China*, p. 244.
9 That's another story, but see Clements, *Rebel Island*, pp. 197–218.
10 Blanchette, *China's New Red Guards*, p. 46.

Strike Black, Sing Red

1 Blanchette, *China's New Red Guards*, p. 4.
2 Lin, *Red Tourism in China*, p. 175.
3 Lin, *Red Tourism in China*, p. 182.
4 Blanchette, *China's New Red Guards*, p. 113.
5 Marquis and Qiao, *Mao and Markets*, p. 123.
6 Marquis and Qiao, *Mao and Markets*, p. 40.
7 Marquis and Qiao, *Mao and Markets*, p. 38.
8 Blanchette, *China's New Red Guards*, p. 155.
9 Chen, *The Secret Listener*, p. 1.
10 Lin, *Red Tourism in China*, p. 15.

Index